Home
GROWN

How to Equip Parents for Spiritual Leadership

KIDMIN NATION LIBRARY

Home Grown: How to Equip Parents for Spiritual Leadership
published by Kidmin Nation
edited by Tina Houser
copyright ©2018

cover design by Vanessa Mendozzi

Contents

Introduction

WHEN YOU TOOK ON THE POSITION as children's pastor, it more than likely had something to do with two facts: you love Jesus, and you love being with kids. You erroneously thought you would spend all your ministry interacting with children. Make no mistake ... children are the target of your evangelistic efforts. But you are only one player in this endeavor.

A huge chunk of your time and energy should go into the people on your ministry team. The larger your team becomes, the less likely you are to be interacting one-on-one with children in their groups. Surprise, you're moving toward administrative responsibilities!

Although you may be under the impression that you and your team make a huge spiritual impression on kids, there is yet another set of players who have an exponentially greater potential for touching these young lives for Jesus—their parents.

Parents are the ones who guide a child's thoughts and actions as the day-to-day challenges and victories happen. They are the ones who are present when those natural teachable moments occur. You and your team can talk about what kids should do if such-and-such happens, but parents can immediately address those thoughts and feelings ... because they are there!

So, are you confused about what your job really is? A children's minister who understands where the real spiritual impact occurs—in the home—will be a cheerleader and equipper to parents, so they can effectively step into those opportunities to speak Jesus into their child's life. Your job has now become very relational as you come alongside the parents or caretakers of the children in your ministry.

This book covers a huge array of topics that you need to educate yourself about so that you can assist parents in fulfilling their role as the primary spiritual leaders to their children. As you read, there will be times when you say to yourself, "We're on the right track!" There will be times when the words remind you of what you already knew, but haven't put into practice. Takes notes. Then, there will be sections where thoughts are shared that you've never considered, and you recognize a "hole" in your ministry. Take more notes. (I did!)

Allow each chapter contributor to encourage you. Let the excitement, of being part of something bigger than yourself, absolutely drench your soul. It will build as you think of what's possible when parents lead their kids daily in God's Word.

Your job description has now aligned itself with what God intended when He addresses families in Deuteronomy 6. We pray that as you read this book, you will not only recognize the challenge, but rise to it—to invest time and resources into the parents of your precious kids.

In His incredible joy,

Tina Houser

Chapter 1

THE UNLIMITED POTENTIAL OF PARTNERING WITH PARENTS

BY PAT CONNER

MOSES WAS ONE OF THE GREAT LEADERS of all time. However, he was not a perfect man or a perfect leader. Though he led God's people to the brink of entering the Promised Land, he was not allowed to enter with them. At this pivotal divide, Moses preached a series of three sermons. His purpose was to instruct the people how God intended for them to live going forward. He chose his words carefully, and God guided Moses as He spoke? The book of Deuteronomy is the record of these sermons delivered by this great leader.

Within the sixth chapter of Deuteronomy, we find very specific instructions for how the faith of children is to be nurtured. Isn't that wonderful? What kids' ministry person wouldn't want to hear these instructions? But wait—the instructions are not for *us* as we teach and minister to children in our churches. These instructions are specifically for parents.

"Hear, O Israel; The Lord our God, the Lord is one. Love the Lord your God with all your heart and with all your soul and with all your strength. These commandments that I give you today are to be upon your hearts. Impress them on your children. Talk about them when you sit at home and when you walk along the road, when you lie down and when you get up" Deuteronomy 6:4-7 (NIV).

Clearly for parents, right? After all, I'm not sitting at home with the children in my ministry. I'm not there when they lie down or when they get up. These directions are great, and as a parent and grandparent, I am challenged and inspired by them. But at first glance they don't seem to be for me as I minister in my church. So what am I to do with them?

Once my heart settles in that these are intentional directions for discipling children, I am thrilled. I'm thrilled that the God of the Universe takes the spiritual nurture of children seriously enough to lay out a clear pathway. I'm thrilled that the family is designated as the institution where that discipling happens. I'm thrilled to think of the potential partnering with parents can bring to our ministry with kids. What are some ways to maximize this potential? I see several.

ENERGIZED MINISTRY

As we have seen, God made it clear that His design and His intention is for parents to have the primary role in discipling their children. They are to live out their faith and pass it on to their children through their example and through their words. There is another part of God's plan. Remember that Moses laid out the plan for the entire community of God's people. Parents are to disciple their children in the context of a loving and supportive community. In today's world that is us—the local church.

If we're honest, we'll admit that the local church has not always followed God's plan as Moses laid it out in Deuteronomy. We, as parents and as ministers, have often fallen back on the flawed thinking that it is simply the job of the church to disciple children. Too many times parents have accepted this idea, and perhaps ministry leaders have allowed parents to abdicate their God-given responsibility. Currently, there is a new understanding in many churches that parents and the church must work together, partnering to make disciples of children.

When we comprehend and begin to obey God's intention, we position ourselves, our families, our church, and our ministries in the best possible place. As we help parents understand and accomplish what God has planned for them to do in the lives of their children, we will see lives change. Many parents will become motivated to follow God's plan. There is work for us to do as we support them, but it's the sort of work that's exciting. It's exciting because it's clearly right. It is clearly God's direction for us. We'll see His blessings in our church, as well as in the lives of parents and children. We'll see them responding to the Lord in new ways. What could be more fun than that?

Our alternative is to try to do the discipling all alone and let the parents do their own "adult" thing. When we do that, we miss what God has planned. Following our own plan for ministry will always be an uphill struggle with diminished results. God made it clear what children need for their hearts to turn toward Him. They need their parents. Their parents need us. Let's figure out how to work together. Along the way, let's not miss the joy and energy of working in the power and the plan of God.

EXPANDED CONVERSATIONS

One of the first things that needs to be addressed as we partner with parents is communication. Have you ever tried to work with someone and you just didn't speak the same language? It's difficult to get on the same page if there's no common language. So let's be sure we are clearly communicating with parents. Use phrases that emphasize the partnership you're striving to achieve. Perhaps a tagline for your ministry will be "Partnering with Parents." If you have stated your values, is partnering or supporting parents one of those values? Be sure you are developing a common language. Use your chosen phrase in email communication or on signs in your ministry area. Have parent meetings where leaders cast the vision of parents themselves discipling children.

All good conversations require at least two-way talking and listening. Conversations with parents are expanded when we signal and practice our willingness to listen. We serve them when we listen to their concerns, when we answer their questions, when we're willing to hear their opinions on how our ministry can be improved. After all, if we are to partner with them, our ministry is their ministry too. This doesn't mean we have to follow every suggestion. It simply means we are willing to listen and have conversations with our partners—parents. And who knows? We may learn something!

One way to expand the conversation is by helping children be a part of the communication. There is no way to count the number of times I've heard variations on this conversation when a parent has just picked up his or her child.

Parent: Did you have a good time in your class?

Child: Yeah.

Parent: What did you do?

Child: Nothing.

Parent: What did you learn?

Child: I can't remember.

Ugh! This doesn't go far to increase the vision for ministry, does it? As ministry leaders, perhaps we can help. We can "practice" or "prep" the children before they're picked up. We can help them expand this conversation by having a pre-conversation. In your wrap-up discussion, talk with the kids about what they have done that day. Ask them to share what they did that was fun. Get them to remind each other what the Bible lesson or the big idea was. We can even help them by giving little "sound bites" that they can easily remember when their parents ask them questions. Wouldn't it be great if the conversation were more like this?

Parent: Did you have a good time in your class?

Child: Yes! (If the answer is "No", we're already doomed!)

Parent: What did you do?

Child: We talked about times when we're afraid.

Parent: Oh really? But did you learn anything?

Child: Yes. We learned what the Bible says. I don't have to be afraid, because God is always with me.

See what we did there? We expanded a conversation between parent and child so that the parent has a basis for a continuing conversation in the days and weeks ahead. By providing parents with tools, we give them a simple way to begin reaching the potential of our partnership.

EQUIPPED AND EMPOWERED PARENTS

I've known very few parents who simply did not care about leading their children spiritually. Sadly, my observation has been that many parents often do not take an active role because they feel inadequate. It's sad to me when a parent phones and says, "My child says he's ready to give his life to Jesus. Could I bring him to talk to you so you can pray with him?" Oh, Mom and Dad! Don't miss this precious privilege. There is no ministry leader who knows your child better than you do. Ministry leaders, let's build a partnership by equipping and empowering parents to do what God has called them to do.

How does this happen? By listening to them, by teaching them, by providing them with resources, and by encouraging them. In our church, we begin by equipping new parents with a required class which precedes Parent/Baby Dedication. In this class, we challenge parents with an explanation that their responsibility is to be the primary faith trainers for their children. Judging from the looks on their faces, I would say their reactions range from shock to fear to absolute joy! We offer suggestions and support.

Of course, this support must continue as baby grows older. Letting parents know what their child is learning is vital. There are many ways to do this. Take-home papers are an old standby, but there must be other ways as well. I like simple conversation guides sent home, emailed, or posted on a website which give parents questions or prompts to use to begin a conversation with their child. These natural conversations are potentially more effective than a sit-down family "devotional" time that may feel unnatural or forced depending on a family's stage of life.

Sometimes parents are "set free" if we can help them see how easy it really is to follow the plan laid out in Deuteronomy 6. In those verses, parents are instructed to talk to the children as they are "walking by the way." For many of us, that would mean as we are driving in the car. Help parents see they can easily have spiritual moments in the car. They can listen to Christian music, memorize scripture together, or have conversations on spiritual questions or issues. This does not have to be overwhelming.

When our children were growing up, my husband had a simple habit which had a big payoff for our family. When we were together in the car, backing down the driveway to leave the house, my husband always said, "Father, thank You for our home." I can't recall that we ever stopped and said, "Now let us pray," and offered a formal prayer of thanksgiving. Instead, by living a life and making consistent simple statements of gratitude, my husband taught a significant spiritual lesson. Many years later, I was visiting my adult daughter. We decided to take her three young children out. As we pulled away from their house, I heard her say, "Thank You, Lord, for our home." She had been discipled simply and effectively by her dad.

Stories such as this have the ability to show parents they already have what it takes to train their children spiritually. It is within their own relationships with the Lord, exactly as Deuteronomy 6 explains.

Of course, there may be times when parents need help. At those times, it is our joy and responsibility to step in and offer suggestions of resources or help from our own experience. This is what a partnership looks like—church and parents working together to train the next generation of Christ-followers. It's a brilliant plan, isn't it? But we do serve a God who created us, who knows us, and who has perfect plans for us. The potential is limitless. I suggest that following God's plan for ministry will bring us great joy.

ENJOYABLE MINISTRY

The truth is that your kids' ministry is not just about kids. It's probably not even primarily about kids, because what you do must also be ministry to parents as they disciple their children. How does that strike you? Does it seem burdensome? I want to suggest that you embrace it joyfully. You have been given the opportunity to make a huge difference in your church. Toss out any talk or thought that you are "just taking care of kids." No! You're at the very heart of the work of the church. You have the delight of watching families grow, helping parents, partnering with them as they do their God-given work. Aren't you just overjoyed at the thought of what God allows you to do?

A thrilling aspect of this type of ministry is watching parents rise to the challenge. I love seeing parents who are intentionally and effectively discipling their children.

On a recent Sunday, I brought a first-time guest to her second grade classroom. She was hesitant, shy, and tearful. As I sat with her, 7-year-old Will came up to us. He reached in his pocket and pulled out a mint, offering it to our new friend. "I'm Will," he said. "Would you like to have this? And you can sit with me." I was so proud of him! Later, I told him so. "Will, thanks so much for being kind to our friend. Thank you for giving her your candy." "Oh," Will replied, "I had to give her the candy. I had two pieces. If you have two of anything, you need to give one of them to someone else. It's what Jesus said to do." What? Of course, I realized right away that he was referring to the passage in Luke 3 where Jesus said if you have two shirts or two coats, give one away. But that passage had not been in our curriculum. Will must have learned it from his parents!

Not long after, I saw Will's parents as we were hanging out in a larger group of people. I told them the story and affirmed them for teaching their children so well. They had joy on their faces, as I'm sure I did. On the faces of the other parents in the group, I saw admiration and determination to continue in discipling their own children. All of us understood that God was at work in Will's life and in his family. This type of joy is multiplied because it is shared with others. I believe this is what ministry is intended to be.

As you follow God's plan for ministry by partnering with parents, your work will be energized, conversations at home and at church will be expanded, parents will be equipped and empowered, and your joy will be increased. A new generation of parents and church members will follow and God's work will go on, just as He planned.

Chapter 2

EQUIP PARENTS FOR FAMILY DISCIPLESHIP

BY STEVEN KNIGHT

ONE OF THE MOST IMPACTFUL MINISTRIES in the church is the ministry to parents. When churches seek to equip parents as the spiritual leaders in their homes, then the parents can take ownership and disciple their children well. Investing in the life of a parent can have a greatly multiplied impact; as parents, they then invest in the lives of their kids.

Sounds exciting, right? The idea sounds great, but actually carrying it out ... well, that can appear overwhelming at first. The key to starting a parent ministry is to "think big, start small." Don't be afraid to dream about what your parent ministry could look like in five years. However, start with a few small steps to get headed in the right direction. For example, is your church doing anything right now that could be adjusted to equip parents? Is there a small family event that you could host at your church or in your community?

As a ministry leader, you are called to serve where God has you right now. Starting small can eventually lead to big things, but the key is that you actually have to take the first few steps. You'll need to determine ways that you can begin equipping parents for family discipleship throughout the week. Think about ways that your church staff can work together to reach parents. Most churches with a successful parent ministry have multiple staff members or key volunteers who include ministry to parents as part of their responsibilities. I would encourage you to not feel the pressure to immediately hire more staff members in order to launch a full-scale parent ministry. Instead, perhaps you and a few other ministry leaders can start by trying out a few small parent ministry initiatives.

Looking for some parent ministry ideas? Take a look at what the Bible says about parenting in Deuteronomy 6. This is frequently referred to as the Shema. Originally written for the nation of Israel during the time of Moses, it gives clear instructions to parents regarding the discipleship of their children—essentially, that this discipleship happens all the time. Notice in vs. 5-6 that loving God requires a full devotion to Him, with our entire being. The words of Scripture should be on our hearts, and parents should teach them to their children, whether that is at home, while they travel, and during everything else they do. The mission of parents is the discipleship of their children during their everyday lives. The verbiage in vs. 8-9 (hand, eyes, doorposts, gates) is a clear reminder that these words should be in the forefront of their minds and should be taught to their children throughout every day.

It can be difficult to determine where to start. If your church doesn't have a plan for parent ministry, then here are some ideas to get you started.

FAMILY TALKS

One of the most effective ways a parent can disciple their kids is to take advantage of time they already have together in their everyday lives—at home, in the car, etc. These environments can be a great place for impactful conversations. At home, they may have time for deeper discussions, while a car trip provides a short amount of time to talk about a specific topic. Through the course of a child's life, a number of topics for discussion and discipleship will naturally come up as they ask questions about life and God. However, these environments are also a great place for parents to initiate conversations with their kids.

For example, if they're driving home from church, they can ask their child about what they learned today in children's church. A common response I've heard from parents is that they don't get much of an answer to this question. What should parents do to get more engagement from their kids? I would recommend two strategies: first, model it for them. They should take time to share with their kids what they learned from a sermon or small group. Secondly, they need to ask good questions that require their kids to think about better answers. Avoid asking "yes" or "no" questions and focus on engaging them in deeper conversations with quality questions. Over time, they'll learn how to engage better in these conversations.

You can equip parents for family discipleship by encouraging them to take advantage of the time they already have and the spiritual topics they're already learning about individually or together. Your role is simply to communicate to parents and give them ideas for ways to initiate and navigate these conversations.

FAMILY DEVOTIONALS

A common form of family discipleship takes place through family devotionals at home. While most parents would agree

17

that family devotionals can be effective, many of them do not know where to find quality material. Ministry leaders can greatly help parents with this task. Often, parents do not feel comfortable selecting theologically-sound and engaging devotionals, and they are very grateful for your recommendations.

Some parents may need your help getting started, since they may have never led a family devotional before. Perhaps you could show a short video that demonstrates what a family devotional looks like. You could either find a video as part of a family devotional curriculum set or create your own video. One time I presented one such video to a group of parents, and it looked like a light bulb turned on for them. These parents realized that they were competent enough to lead a family devotional themselves! I suspect they also felt better knowing that most other families have energetic kids and that it took some effort to get everyone in the same room together and focused on the devotional.

PARTNERING WITH KIDS' MINISTRY AND STUDENT MINISTRY

With a little extra work, every kids' ministry and student ministry can equip parents for family discipleship throughout the week. Many churches provide a handout or send an email with a family devotional that is related to the curriculum that the kids' ministry or student ministry is currently teaching. Most curriculum providers have realized the impact that these devotionals can have, so they've started providing family devotional resources along with the curriculum. If some families already have an established family devotional time during the week, then using this curriculum resource could be a good way for a parent to connect directly with a child and have a spiritual conversation together weekly.

I recommend sending family devotionals via email using an email service (like MailChimp). Once you've spent a few hours learning how to use the email service system, it should take less than an hour each week to create the email with a family devotional in it. One hour a week is a small time investment for a significant impact. If you want to get more parents on board with these devotionals from the beginning, consider asking your senior pastor to share about the devotionals on a Sunday morning.

If your church has small groups in kids' ministry or student ministry, then you can greatly increase the discipleship impact of the parents and small group leaders by getting them in the same room with each other and talking about the spiritual growth of their kids. One of my favorite ways to open up these conversations is to invite parents and small group leaders to a coffee conversation where you provide a few short questions that the parents and small group leaders can talk through. Ultimately, this helps both the parents and the small group leaders to more effectively disciple the kids by giving them a better assessment of their child's level of spiritual maturity and growth areas.

FAMILY EVENTS

As a ministry leader, you have the opportunity to create family events that bring families together and help them learn how they can spend meaningful time together creating memories, having important conversations, and enjoying time with each other. These events can include fun activities, discipleship-oriented activities, memorable activities—wherever your imagination takes you. (Check out the Family Event section of this book for ideas.)

FAMILY SERVE OPPORTUNITIES

An easy way to equip parents in your church is to provide them with opportunities for their families to serve together. Find current outreach opportunities in your church that families can do together or do some research for opportunities in your local community. Some non-profit ministries have these opportunities, but you may have to contact them directly to find out about them. Find ways for families to serve together, then clearly communicate those opportunities to the rest of your church.

PARENTING CLASSES

If you're looking for ways to equip parents concerning specific topics or life stages, then holding a parenting class can be a very effective way to educate them. A parenting class has the advantage of being able to focus on specific topics like parenting and technology, parenting and finances, parenting in a sexualized culture, etc. Parents can then take what they've learned and apply it to their parenting skills and family discipleship conversations. These classes can be taught by a live teacher or by using a video teaching series.

A development in recent years in North America has been the rise of family milestones classes. There are several milestones strategies out there and each one focuses on helping parents disciple children, giving specific instructions to them, and celebrating big moments with them—birth through adulthood. While this parenting ministry initiative takes more effort than most of the ideas noted here, it can also be one of the most effective ways to equip parents for family discipleship. The key to launching these classes successfully is to build a team of teachers who can help your ministry staff lead each of the classes.

CHURCH SCHEDULING FOR FAMILIES

One of the best ways that you can help equip parents is to make sure you give them the gift of time. Take a look at your church calendar. For a family of five, do your church's ministry events take up their entire week? While some families have problems with overcommitting to other activities during the week, some families will show up every time your church opens the doors.

A simple way to help families slow down their busy lives is to schedule your church's ministry events in a way that reduces the strain on families' calendars. Can you schedule some of the kids, students, and adult ministry gatherings at the same time? Can you schedule special events close to the same time and location, so that parents only have to drop their kids off at one location?

To achieve this level of scheduling, it will usually require planning up to a year in advance. If your ministry team creates their ministry calendar for next year in advance, then this goal is easily within reach. If your ministry team does not plan that far out yet, then you could become a catalyst for other ministries to begin working together to plan coordinated ministry times that free up more time for families.

PARENT NEWSLETTERS

One of my favorite methods for equipping parents is a parent newsletter. In these newsletters, you can add recommendations for your favorite parenting resources. A parent newsletter gives you the opportunity to share about different outreach opportunities and parenting events that your church will be involved in. You can also add some parenting testimonials in order to encourage other parents ... and yes, parents will welcome all the encouragement they can get! If you have the time, I would also recommend linking to several online parenting articles that address different ages of children or specific life circumstances.

If you start this initiative, make sure you pace yourself and find a sustainable frequency for creating these newsletters. In most churches, creating a monthly parent newsletter is an attainable goal. Regularly sending them out will also function as small reminders to parents about their role in discipling their kids. While not every parent will read your newsletters, you can still reach some of them and further equip them with tools for family discipleship.

CHURCH WEBSITE: PARENT RESOURCE CENTER

Most parents are interested in parenting resources that address their specific circumstances or their child's life stages, but many of them don't know how to find these resources. Some parents do not feel educated enough to discern which resources are biblically-sound and practical. Creating simple lists of helpful books, websites, articles, and podcasts can be very helpful for parents. There are also some ministry resource providers who create packages of parent resources that you can purchase and give to all the parents in your church. Regardless of which option you choose, you can use your church's website to create an easy-to-access location for all of your recommended parenting resources. If you're not sure where to start, just search online for the parent ministry webpages of other churches, and you'll find a few ideas for your own church.

CONCLUSION

With a little bit of effort and intentionality, you can make a great impact and equip the parents in your church with resources and opportunities for family discipleship throughout the week. Just remember—THINK BIG, START SMALL. Equipping parents to disciple their children can have a multiplying impact that can radically change the church and community. Children will grow in their relationship with Christ and begin making an eternal impact themselves in your church, in your community, and around the world.

Chapter 3

STAND ON THE AUTHORITY OF GOD'S WORD

BY AMBER PIKE

L ET'S FACE IT, CHURCH NO LONGER PLAYS the same role in the lives of families as it did in years gone by. The hours a church has to invest in and minister to a child is shrinking. On average, with only one hour a week to minister to a child inside the church, it's obvious that parents play a pivotal role in the faith development of a child. The last decade has brought to everyone's attention what family ministry is and why it is important. Whether your church has an official "family ministry" or not, the church needs to be educating and equipping parents to minister to their children at home.

Just as the church's foundation is built on Christ and His Word, the foundation for parents and families needs to be on the authority of God's Word. If you do not want to lose this generation of children, parents need to be equipped to stand on the authority of God's Word at home.

Inform parents of the Bible's ultimate authority. After parents begin to study and learn about the Bible, they then need to be informed that God's Word is the ultimate authority and what that looks like in their lives.

There are five simple facts that break down how to stand on the authority of God's Word.

1. Know that the Bible is inspired by God.
2. Believe that the Word of God is true, free from mistakes and errors.
3. Realize that ALL Scripture is useful for teaching, correcting, training in righteousness, and reproof.
4. Do not add to, take away from, or pick and choose which parts of the Bible you follow.
5. Stand on the authority of God's Word, by knowing what's in it!

Educate parents on the dangers of not standing on the authority of God's Word. Just telling parents that they should rely on the Bible's authority isn't good enough. They need to know why they should. Why will it benefit their lives? What dangers do they face if they do not?

Statistics show that two-thirds of young people are leaving the church, never to return. During their research, the Barna Group discovered that a major contributing factor to this epidemic is the doubting of God's Word. When you begin to doubt God's Word, it can eventually lead to doubting your need for the Savior. If you want your children to have authentic, life-long relationships with Christ, you must start with the Word of God as your foundation.

Equip parents with the resources they need. Let's face it, parenting can be tough. Parenting with eternity in mind can be even more intimidating. Many parents feel overwhelmed with the idea that they are the ones who are supposed to be leading their children to Christ and training them in the faith. For some, the thought of simply praying with their child is so overwhelming that they don't even attempt it. Telling parents they need to stand on the authority of God's Word isn't enough. We need to give them practical resources they can use.

1. Bible-based curriculum and resources that show the Bible as one big redemption story

Is the curriculum you use at church deeply rooted in the Scripture? Does it stand on the authority of God's Word? Is each lesson jumping around to a different Bible account each week, or is it chronological, showing children (and parents through them) how the Bible fits together and God's plan for redemption?

Parents need an understanding of the Bible as one, big redemption story. Knowing that Noah built the ark and Paul was shipwrecked isn't enough. The Bible is not just a bunch of random stories. From creation to consummation, God's Word tells us of our need for a Savior (Old Testament) and the fulfillment of that promise (New Testament).

Make sure the curriculum you use, and the take-home resources you send, show parents the authority of God in the Scriptures. The Bible is a true account of the history of the world—the story of God's redeeming love and grace.

2. Family experiences and take-homes that encourage being in God's Word

Assuming that all parents know how to plan an at-home worship service or even that all parents spend time reading the Bible with their children is not a safe bet. Provide your parents with weekly, monthly, or quarterly resources that get them diving into God's Word. Some great ideas for experiences and resources for the home are:

- A weekly take-home (paper or digital) that provides scriptures for families to read together based on their lesson. (Many companies provide this resource with their curriculums.)
- Lent, Thanksgiving, and Advent family kits or devotions
- A list of scriptures to pray over their child for: the start of school, problem areas, general growth
- Devotion books that go along with your camp or VBS theme (for the child or the family)
- Scripture memory cards
- Bibles, devotion books, and Bible studies for milestone events, such as birth, salvation, and baptism
- Any resource that you can put into parents' hands (or their inbox) that encourages them and tells them how to dive into God's Word with their kids

3. Practical tips and tools to use in everyday life

What tips and tools can you give parents to make the authority of the Bible real in their lives? Think about these areas where the authority of God's Word can be applied.

- The movies and shows we watch
- The books we read
- The music we listen to
- The choices we make

A lot of things we put into our bodies do not honor God or line up with what His Word says. How can you equip parents for this? Are there resources you can provide parents? For books/movies/shows that do not honor God, provide parents with the scripture references to start a discussion at home. This could be very beneficial. Provide parents with sources of great, new Christian entertainment (or even giving them samples if your budget allows) is another great option.

4. Teach parents how to discipline from a biblical foundation.

God's Word is full of parenting advice, even on how children are to be disciplined. When parenting biblically—standing on the authority of God's Word—the Bible should be the source of discipline. The goal is not to merely change a child's behavior, but to change their heart—course correction, not behavior modification. Unless you want a child behaving just because you tell them to (or to avoid punishment), parents need to use the Bible to correct a child's heart.

Teach parenting workshops or provide parents with resources to direct them how to discipline their children from a biblical basis. Telling a child not to lie, not because they will avoid punishment, but because God's Word commands us not to, has a greater kingdom effect. Disciplining with the authority of God's Word cannot just change a child's behavior, but it needs to change their heart.

5. Encourage the parents in your ministry.

Parenting is tough. From sleepless nights soothing a newborn to worrying through their adolescent years, there is no end to parents' worry. "Did I make the right choice?" "Was I too hard on them?" "Have I done enough to prepare them?"

Parents need encouragement from you. They need more than just being told they are doing a good job or what a great kid they have. Consistently remind them of the benefits of parenting with God's Word as the ultimate authority in their lives. Yes, parents want to raise good, successful children. But more than that, godly parents want to raise children who become successful followers of Christ.

Raising children who have an authentic, lifelong relationship with Christ, starts with the Word of God. Encourage the parents in your ministry to know God's Word, to live out His commands in their own lives, and to lead their children based on the Word of God. He is the ultimate authority in all areas of our lives, including how we parent the children He has blessed us with!

Chapter 4

PUT AWAY YOUR WHISTLE AND PICK UP YOUR POMPOMS

BY BRITTANY NELSON

IN DEUTERONOMY 6 AND 11, THE BIBLE encourages parents to obey God's laws and pass them on to their children during everyday activities: *"Talk about them when you sit at home and when you walk along the road, when you lie down and when you get up"* Deut. 6:7, 11:19 (NIV). Nearly every family ministry resource will tell you that part of our role as kidmin leaders includes empowering parents to be the primary disciplers of their children. But sometimes our approach to equipping parents can actually have the opposite result of what we want.

In my early years of ministry, I provided resources about how to be the best parent and what the "Christian parent" should be doing in their home, but I quickly learned that sometimes these types of resources created more guilt and shame than encouragement or advice. Moms did not feel they could live up to all of the resources I was providing, and it left them feeling overwhelmed. I was inadvertently becoming like the teachers of the law in Luke 11:46 who *"load people down with burdens they can hardly carry"* (NIV). Yikes! That was definitely not my goal.

Since then, I have learned to switch my mentality as a children's pastor from parent coach to parent cheerleader. It may seem like semantics, but this shift creates a brand new mindset to interacting with parents and completely changes your approach to supporting them in their day-to-day lives.

So what's the difference?

A coach is someone who instructs or trains, who offers advice on how to improve.

A cheerleader is an enthusiastic and vocal supporter of what someone is already doing.

The difference lies in the relationship and the result. Yes, coaches encourage their players, but they also come with a set of expectations that players must achieve. A cheerleader supports players no matter their performance and inspires them to keep going at every step of the way. Being a parent cheerleader rather than a parent coach communicates to parents that no matter what, you are there to help them draw their children and their families closer to God. When you're a parent cheerleader, you allow parents to claim ownership of the faith formation of their children, positioning you to support them along the way.

My best friend recently had her first child, and what a time of celebration, joy, and exhaustion it has been. I asked her about the most challenging aspect of motherhood so far, and her response surprised me. I expected an answer that referred to sleepless nights, poopy diapers, or the sudden lack of personal time. But her answer went much deeper: "There are so many different voices that tell you how to be the best parent, and sometimes they contradict each other. I feel like no matter what I do, someone is judging me for my parenting choices or trying to tell me what I'm doing wrong so I can improve."

Parents are already bombarded with more do's and don'ts than they can handle. Rather than being another voice in the world that tells families what they should and shouldn't be, our role as children's ministry leaders should be to find out what parents are doing and come alongside them to be a support in that.

KNOW WHO YOU'RE CHEERING FOR

So how do we switch our approach from coach to cheerleader? The bottom line is if we're going to support parents in their everyday lives, we have to be part of their everyday lives. So start with them. What are the challenges that the parents in your ministry and your community face?

Based on my experiences and conversations, the top challenge that families in my ministry face is a too-busy schedule. When surveyed, the moms in my ministry all stated feeling overwhelmed with the demanding pressures and expectations they face for themselves, their kids, and their families as a whole. This busyness offers the greatest challenge because moms constantly feel inadequate at parenting their kids, and not just in spiritual terms but in all areas of life. Instead of talking *at* parents, we must listen *to* them, and find out what their challenges are so we can provide relevant and applicable support.

One of the best ways to find out about the challenges parents in your ministry face is to spend time with them. Let's get out of our offices and meet parents for coffee, lunch, or even a walk around the block. I have made it a goal to meet with at least one mom a week, with no other purpose than to hear about her life—the struggles, the joys, the face-palms, and everything in between. Sometimes the kids come along and play while we talk, and sometimes I meet with them at their homes while the kids are napping. Some of my most effective moments of ministering to parents has happened during these times.

If you are a bi-vocational or volunteer children's pastor or if your ministry serves several hundred families, then I know your schedule may not allow weekly coffee dates. Another practical alternative is to create a parent council. A parent council is a group of 8-10 parents of your choosing that meets regularly to provide feedback, guidance, and input on the children's ministry. Creating this advisory board communicates to parents that it's okay to talk to you about both the good and the bad. I'd much rather have my parent council complain to me about the poor organization at the Preschool Playdate than have all the parents complaining to each other! I set up a parent council in my second year of ministry and have loved it ever since. They met quarterly, and I emailed them when I had a question about something that I wanted their input on but didn't require an entire meeting. A parent council reminds parents that it's more about them than about you and sets you up to be a parent cheerleader.

Another excellent way to stay in touch with the families in your ministry is through social media platforms like Twitter, Instagram, and especially Facebook. Now more than ever, we can find out about what's going on in someone's life without actually having to talk to them. And while the implications of this change are vast, one positive is that we can quickly receive updates on the lives of the families in our ministry. Use Facebook to see their family outings, celebrations, grievances, and even to remember parents' birthdays.

To cheer parents on, we have to know what parents are doing, and that involves closing our mouths and opening our ears as parents share their thoughts, fears, and challenges.

CHEER THEM ON

Once we know what parents need, how do we practically encourage them? What are some ways we can help them solve

PUT AWAY YOUR WHISTLE AND PICK UP YOUR POMPOMS

the challenges they face and support them in their efforts to *"train up a child in the way he should go"* Proverbs 22:6 (NASB).

Pray. This one really should be a no-brainer in our line of work. Let's get on our knees and go to battle for the parents and families we serve. Pray specifically and purposely for their needs, and ask God to move in the hearts and minds of the parents you serve. Pray for your role in the discipling of their children, and ask God to help you be a parent cheerleader and an encourager. Bonus: tell parents you're thinking of them and praying for them just as often as you say the same thing to their children.

Be a library of resources. We don't have to become experts in knowledge if we are experts in resources. Be familiar with the resources available for parents so when they ask, you can give them a short answer that still provides all the information they need. Another source of knowledge for parents could include resources more specific to your ministry, such as a monthly calendar of Sunday's Bible stories that parents can read at home with their children before coming to church. Weekly text messages with discussion questions for meal times or short examples of how to use various daily routines (bath time, brushing teeth, etc.) for a faith conversation may also be helpful resources. By providing ways that allow kids and families to interact with Bible stories from Sunday mornings throughout the week, ministry leaders essentially enable families to *"tie them [the stories] as symbols on your hands and bind them on your foreheads"* Deut. 6:8 (NIV).

Take the pressure off. As you're building your library of resources, remind parents that these resources are available as support, not as expectations. One of the most common statements I hear from parents in my ministry is a feeling of intense pressure that every at-home faith conversation must be profoundly spiritual and sacred. I like to remind parents that faith development at home does not always require in-depth Bible studies; Deuteronomy 6 and 11 show us that the in-between moments of travel, sharing meals, and bedtime and morning routines can all provide time for conversations about God. Offering a variety of ideas that are easy for parents to use at home and communicating their simplicity helps eliminate the pressure some parents may feel. Providing multiple solutions allows parents to choose which approaches will work best for their family. Rather than adding to the anxiety and making parents feel guilty for their constrained time, let's help them find ways to incorporate moments with God into their schedules. Some of you may think that God should take priority over anything else on the calendar, and I agree with you. But the reality is that families' schedules don't always reflect that priority, and if we choose to criticize, judge, or make them feel guilty, we'll end up pushing families further from the church instead of drawing them closer.

Create a realistic calendar. An easy way to relieve some pressure is to evaluate your calendar. Rather than adding commitments with more events and expectations, find activities families are already doing and help them tie those into God's Word. Are a majority of the children in your ministry part of the school talent show? Use that as a way to talk about spiritual gifts and the talents God has given us. Is the town hosting a glowing lantern event the same night you wanted to host the Easter Egg Hunt? Skip the egg hunt this year to join the community in their lantern-making, and talk about how Jesus is the light of the world. Bottom line: rather than creating a completely separate calendar for your ministry that just becomes one more thing on each families' to-do list, use the community and school calendars to guide your special events planning.

It's also important to know the seasons of busy-ness for the families in your ministry. As much as we'd love it if the families in our church only had our events on their calendar, the reality is they have commitments (a lot of them) outside of our ministries. My families have asked for no extra events past the first weekend of December until after Christmas and from the beginning of May until after school gets out. Those two months are jam-packed with school activities and extracurriculars, so I scale back on the commitments at church during those times.

Be available. One of the perks of our job is that we have a flexible schedule, so let's use that to our advantage! When you hear of a parent in need, step in. I received a text one afternoon that one of my families was in the ER because their kindergartener hit her head on the playground and was complaining that she could no longer see. Both parents were in the ER with the kindergartener and their 2-year-old daughter. I put down the craft I was prepping for Sunday, drove to the hospital, and took the 2-year-old to the playground so Mom and Dad could focus on their injured child. Once we heard that the family was heading home, we stopped by the grocery store to pick up dinner for them. The mother reiterated several times how much it meant to her that I stepped in during a crisis moment. Being available to help in the big moments opened doors for me to impact the little moments too. (And don't worry, the kindergartener was okay.)

Find ways to serve them and step into their world. Parents often serve in our ministries as volunteers, coordinators, and more, so we should look for ways to serve in their worlds, too. One year, I offered to help one of my volunteers set up her third grade classroom before school started, and she later told me that my offer to help made her feel valued and appreciated as a volunteer. Do one of the moms in your ministry lead an exercise class? Join in one day and then take her out for a post-workout meal. Meet a parent at work with a tasty lunch in tow, or serve a parent by picking up their child from preschool that day for an afternoon at the park so Mom has some time to herself. No matter what it looks like, let's commit to stepping out of our church world and into the lives of the parents we serve.

Provide car time solutions. The vehicle is quickly replacing the dinner table as the family's gathering place while families jet between soccer practices, dance rehearsals, piano lessons, and church. We can help parents use that time in the car-rider line before school to speak blessings over their children or utilize the drive to soccer practice as a way to ask about the child's day. Or make it even simpler and create a Spotify playlist of your ministry's favorite worship songs so families can listen to it in the car. For some of our special events like VBS and church-wide weekend retreats, I like to create podcasts about that day's lesson for families to listen to or provide conversation starters.

Connect parents with other parents. Create communities and remind parents they are not alone. Helping parents connect with others in the same stage of life and a different stage of life helps remedy the lack of competence many parents feel. Whether it's small groups, preschool playdates, family events, Facebook groups, or something else, incorporate ways for parents to build relationships with other parents so they have a whole team of people cheering them on.

PICK UP YOUR POMPOMS

Ultimately, we want to establish an "open door" culture within our ministries so that parents know that we are on their team and available for support, practical encouragement, or even just a listening ear. So when it comes to parents, put away your whistle and pick up your pompoms. Be a cheerleader and a champion of the parents in your ministry.

Chapter 5

KEEP IN TOUCH WITH PARENTS

BY LUCINDA GIBSON

COMMUNICATING WITH PARENTS is essential in kids' ministry. The reality is, kids are dependent on their parents. Parents hold the final say in whether their children attend our weekly programming and special events. Therefore, it's vital for parents to know what's going on within our ministries. The age-old question then is: "How do we communicate effectively to parents?" Here are some hacks to keep in mind.

KNOW WHAT YOU NEED TO SAY AND SAY ONLY THAT

First of all, you need to know exactly what you're trying to communicate. Parents today are raising kids in a rush-rush world. They are busy. If our communication is wordy and cumbersome to wade through, it's likely they will miss the details. Ask yourself what is the "must know" information. What do parents need to know? Time, ages, location, how to register. Then ask yourself, "How do I best convey this information in a clear, succinct manner?"

LEARN THE COMMUNICATION LANGUAGES OF PARENTS, AND SPEAK ALL OF THEM

We cannot pick just one method of communication and expect to be effective in reaching all our parents. The parents in your ministry are as diverse as the kids. You may have grandparents raising kids in your ministry who do not have a presence on social media. Church bulletins, newsletters, and flyers work well for this group. You also most likely have parents, like myself, who feel overwhelmed with the number of papers that come home from school, church, and other activities. I can never find the paper I need when I need to go back and get the details. I love being able to access the information on a website, or in a text, at the click of a button. Make sure clear information is readily available and easy to find on your website. Figure out which social media outlets your parents use regularly. We've found one of our best modes of advertising is to create an event on Facebook. Our members are then able to share the event with their Facebook friends to spread the news far and wide. Yet I know of at least one mom in my ministry who has chosen not to be part of Facebook but is on Twitter instead. Therefore, I know I need to use both means of communication.

As technology advances so does our means of communicating. Make graphic announcements visually appealing and to the point. You can use websites such as Adobe Spark and Canva to almost effortlessly make graphics that are up-to-date and eye-catching. Video is also very trendy. A wordy post that requires someone to take the time to read may be bypassed, but a video may be clicked just out of curiosity. One of my friends recently shared a video on Facebook by a family pastor. I curiously clicked on it. He talked about a resource for families. The video was short and sweet and to the point. It had been shot in his office on his cell phone or computer, but it communicated this resource and that he cared about helping families. Communicate in a variety of ways to have the maximum impact.

MAKE A COMMUNICATION PLAN

Once you've decided what you want to communicate and you've listed all the different avenues you need to use for that communication, it can be overwhelming. Make a communication plan to help you successfully get the word out. Find and use automation tools that make the job even easier. You can use post scheduling tools such as Hootsuite or Buffer to schedule posts on social media. Email programs such as MailChimp allow you to send out group emails that are personalized. They can be typed out ahead of time and scheduled when to be sent. Group messaging apps such as Remind let you schedule texts. These incredible tools, and others of this type, help you set aside one block of time and prepare all of the promotions for an event or program ... and be done.

Make a plan to spread out information on different platforms so that parents who use more than one platform are not hit with the same information on all platforms at the same time. Instead, they will receive several reminders throughout the span of a few days. I use a Sunday morning curriculum that comes with a great resource of talking points for each week in the form of two Tweets, one Facebook post, and an email body that I can copy and paste. Each week I schedule these posts and emails to go out in the days leading up to Sunday, Sunday afternoon, and Monday morning. With these posts, my hope is that it will inspire conversations between children and their parents to further the discussion of what they learned at church. I set aside a couple of hours the month before a new quarter and schedule all the Facebook and Twitter communications in Hootsuite for the quarter. I also begin an email for each week of the quarter in MailChimp with the email body provided by the curriculum. Then, each week I'm able to quickly add graphic announcements to the bottom of the email and schedule it to my subscribers' inboxes first thing Monday morning.

When I have events, I start by making graphic announcements in a program like Adobe Spark or Canva. From those graphics I schedule tweets, Facebook posts, and text spread out with increasing frequency as events and deadlines draw near. I send the graphic to our music minister to add to our announcement slide. I print posters to hang and flyers to hand out. I add info to our church website or put it on my calendar on the date it needs to be added. All of my promotions match across the board. As the event approaches, all the promotions happen automatically. I don't have to remember to take a moment Saturday afternoon in the middle of time with my family to send a reminder about an event the next day. It just happens!

Don't just communicate ... connect.

A vital part of our ministry to kids is connection. We're building relationships in hope of being able to share Jesus with these kids and walk alongside them in this journey we call life. We also need to connect and build relationships with their parents. This is total speculation on my part, but I believe the more parents believe that I truly care about and love their children, the more they want them to be part of what happens in my ministry, and the more likely they are to open my communications.

Take time to build that relationship and help parents know just how much you care about their child. Don't miss the chance to speak to parents when they pick up their child. Share something funny that happened that morning. If a child has mentioned they are headed out of town, wish the parents a safe journey. Let the parents know you're praying for the sick grandparent their child mentioned in prayer time. Snap a picture of two sweet friends working together in Sunday school and send the picture to their moms by text. Having a super hero night? Take lots of pictures. Pick out a good one of each kid and email it to their parents. Having a nerf war? Take many pictures. Try to get some of each child. Make a video and share with parents so they can glimpse the fun their kids had. When one of your kids says something that has you chuckling a few days later, send a quick text to the parents telling them how much joy their child brings to your life.

Find ways to sincerely praise the children in your ministry to their parents. As a parent it means the world to hear that someone else enjoys your child, especially when it's trying at home and parents are struggling to feel successful at this parenting thing.

COMMUNICATE YOUR WHY

If you want your parents to buy in to the fact that your ministry is something that will add value to their family's life, you need to help them see the "why" behind what you are doing. We're not gathering together and teaching kids Sunday school week in and week out for no reason. It has great purpose!

In today's culture many things are pulling at families for their time and attention. If we want families to put having their children as a part of our ministries high on their priority list, we have to help them see the value in it. Shoot a short video sharing your heart behind the reason you feel your new series on the Armor of God is important for their kids to learn about. When you read new research that drives you to refocus on kids being in the Word, share those statistics with parents. Help parents see the value your ministry can bring to their family. Help them understand why you do what you do.

Here's what it boils down to—COMMUNICATE! Parents are not mind readers. Maybe the event you're planning is one that happens the same every year. Don't forget you have new people who were not there last year. Always communicate the facts each time, and do it in a variety of ways. Through many avenues you can reach many people. Help parents know what's happening in your ministry, but above all, help parents understand that their children are wanted, loved, and accepted in your ministry.

Chapter 6

SHIFT FOCUS

BY MAKINNA MORRISON

W HEN SEARCHING FOR A CHURCH many families feel overwhelmed. How can you as a kids' ministry leader create an environment that makes new families feel welcome and comfortable? In a survey of over 50 families, the top three things they look for in a church are: a safe environment, strong biblical teaching, and energetic volunteers and staff. The key to creating a family-friendly church is held within these three ideas.

SAFE ENVIRONMENT

The first thing parents want to know when entering a new church is how their children will be kept safe. When a parent knows their child is safe, they can attend church with peace of mind. So, how do you create a safe environment? There are many different aspects of your church that need to be checked to ensure a safe family environment is present.

Volunteers. How do you ensure that your volunteers are equipped to serve? One way to prepare volunteers is through safety training. Training should include background checks, instructions on how to handle emergency situations, fire and tornado plans, and general training on parent interaction. When volunteers are trained, they are more likely to handle situations properly in the case of a crisis. By training your volunteers, you can be confident that your staff knows how to handle all situations and will take excellent care of each child. This confidence helps parents feel secure in leaving their most precious belongings in the hands of strangers.

Registration. Do you have a structured system for collecting information on new children in your church? If not, this is an important security measure that you should consider investing in. At any moment, a child may enter your care, and you need to collect information on this child. Having a secure registration system allows parents to provide contact information, allergies, and special needs. Some registration systems print name tags for all children, and the parents receive a corresponding security tag for pick-up purposes. This added level of security is sure to calm the nerves of a parent leaving their child for the first time. It is vital to be able to assure a parent that his or her child will leave the children's department with the correct person.

Location. You wouldn't buy a new house without seeing the inside first, right? We also wouldn't send our children to a preschool without taking a tour. So, why do we expect parents to hand over their children to us without showing them the area their children will be in? One mom explained her experience saying, "I visited a church where kids were obviously not welcome in the adult worship service; however, as a visitor, I was not comfortable dropping my child in a place with which I was unfamiliar and especially with adults I had never laid eyes on before. She was 3 at the time." The key to making a family feel welcome lies in how you welcome them the first time they come! Invite new parents to tour the facilities. You can even assign this job to a volunteer who is skilled in communication but does not feel comfortable teaching. Take the time to walk the parents and child through the children's area, showing them everywhere their child will visit, and the teacher responsible for the well-being of the child. This is also a great opportunity for leaders to get to know the parents and for the parents to ask specific questions. This may even be an awesome opportunity to share the vision and goals of your ministry!

Safety is so important. Many families will not even consider a church where they do not feel safe leaving their children. Making each family feel safe in your church may look different since each family has very different needs. However, when you begin to examine your ministry you may find that you've not put proper precautionary safety measures into place. Possibly, you think that you have the proper procedures in place, but you have not made these a priority. Parents, leaders, and staff all need to be on the same team when it comes to safety. Everyone should feel confident in how to answer safety questions from guests, how to handle emergency situations, and who to contact if necessary. Posting these procedures in each classroom area may also be helpful. Make safety a priority; families will appreciate the extra work it takes.

STRONG BIBLICAL TEACHING

What you are teaching is important, but communicating what you are teaching to parents is just as crucial. Parents want to know that their children are learning the Word of God. They want to know that your ministry is more than a babysitting service. The best way to do this is to be completely transparent! You can implement this in your church in many different ways. One practical way is by setting up a parent communication wall or board. Use this to post the topic of your lessons weekly. You can also post announcements, calendars, and take-home resources here. This is a quick and simple way to show your parents weekly what their child is learning. Another easy way is to be sure that your ministry focuses on strong biblical teaching is to convey this to parents through your mission statement. Fun is great, and there is a time and place for it, but it's not all about fun. Your mission statement should incorporate and focus on the most important parts of your ministry.

Do not do this: "Our ministry is a fun, energetic, and safe environment where kids can learn about Jesus."

Do this instead: "Our children's ministry focuses on helping your child grow spiritually through strong biblical teaching, all while they learn in a fun and safe environment."

The difference in these two statements is the focus! So, let me ask, what are you focused on? Are you focused on making sure that kids in your ministry have fun? Changing your focus away from fun may be difficult, but the results are remarkable. Here are four practical ways to shift your focus from fun to faith.

Use your time wisely. How many times have you finished a lesson early and used games, coloring, or toys to fill the extra time? We're all guilty of it, but it's time to change this mindset. The amount of time you have with each child is limited. Therefore, you should be good stewards of this time and use every minute to help the children in your ministry grow. How can you utilize these precious minutes, though, when so much of your planning time is dedicated to other things? I've found that the best thing is taking a free day once every month and creating 5-10 extra materials. These materials may include games, Bible drills, or other activities that are intentional and purposeful. By doing this, you can have extra materials ready to use at all times, but instead of mindless movement, the kids are participating in activities that help them grow spiritually!

Plan your lessons with intention. Do you plan your lessons around the activity you want to do, the game you want to play, or even the cute idea you found on Pinterest? I love Pinterest as much as the next person, but it's not the best place to start in lesson planning. Instead, plan your lessons in reverse! Start planning your lessons with your end goal in mind. Set a specific goal for your children and identify what you want them to take away from the lesson. Then, seek out games, activities, and other fun things to incorporate into your lesson. When you plan your lesson backwards, with the end goal in mind, you're much more intentional about what you're teaching. Know what you want your students to learn, and be intentional about conveying that idea throughout the time you're with the children.

Be a role model. Be sure that you're not only teaching things that align with God's Word, but that you're living out these ideas each day. We've all heard the saying "Children are like sponges," but it doesn't just apply to your words. They soak up everything you say and DO! So, make sure that your life is a good example for them. Parents will trust you more when they see that you live by what you teach.

Let the parents lead. Parents spend exponentially more time with their children than children's ministers do, so why are we trying to take them out of discipleship? Just as much as you are a role model for the children you teach, so are their parents, grandparents, and other family members. Allow parents to be a part of this by sending home questions to follow up on the lesson each week or encouraging children to worship corporately with their families.

It's time to evaluate where your focus lies. Are you focusing on winning kids to your ministry through fun games, activities, prizes, lights, and cool music? Or, instead, are you focusing on winning kids for Jesus through strong biblical teaching, being an example, and not wasting one second of the precious time you get with them? Take a moment to sit down with trusted peers and evaluate each individual part of your ministry and the role it plays in winning kids to Christ. You may see that some aspects of your ministry are simply there for entertainment, fun, or just because "it's the way we've always done it."

Fun is good! Fun keeps kids focused, fun helps kids express themselves, fun has a purpose and a place, but it's time to be intentional and create churches that are focused on faith over fun. Together with parents, create a safe and fun environment where children truly learn about and encounter the Savior.

ENERGETIC VOLUNTEERS AND STAFF

I've heard it a million times, "You are such a special person for working with kids." Often, I don't even know how to respond. I realize that these people mean well, but they are totally missing the point. Working in kids' ministry is not a chore or a burden; it is a passion! However, we're doing a poor job of conveying this passion to the families who enter our churches. One parent put it this way: "I wish that our children's director would be passionate about ministry and not just look at it as a job or a to-do list."

Parents view children's ministry workers as miserable and burdened by their children. When you yourself are not excited about the work you're doing, how can you expect parents and children to be excited? Parents and kids will react to your energy! Make sure that parents and kids see your excitement and passion. Think of each interaction with a family as an interview for a job. Who do you believe would be chosen for the job of discipling their child? Would they choose someone who is boring, mundane, and seems to be miserable, or someone who is bubbly, energetic, and passionate about their work. People will consistently gravitate towards the person with passion and energy.

Besides conveying your excitement to new families, include them in the awesome things that you have going on. Share your personal story with them, and let them see where your heart is. Being vulnerable is a big part of this, and it can be tough, but being genuine is key. You do not have to be perfect! Simply show families that you care.

Approach each family you meet with love. Love is the one strand that ties every suggestion and strategy in this chapter together. Love families enough to calm their fears, answer their questions, and protect their children. Love the Gospel in a way that it is undoubtedly the focus of every moment spent with children in your ministry. Love serving so much that your passion and excitement is evident in every action you take and every word you speak. Welcome every person with open arms.

When asked why some families visited a church and never returned, many parents felt ostracized and unwelcome. One mother stated, "My daughter is on the autism spectrum. She always had separation anxiety when I dropped her off. I always felt like the workers viewed it as a discipline issue and would distance themselves, instead of trying to help us through it." Another parent explained, "As a single parent, I really have yet to find a church home where I feel completely welcome. It's all about traditional family—mom, dad, and kids—in every church I've been to. It may be the majority of families at a church, but not all of them, and it alienates those of us who aren't." These experiences display the opposite of love.

Some families may be struggling financially. The single mother may have been in an abusive relationship. The child who smells funny may have parents who do not care. The family who shows up 20 minutes late may have car trouble. Welcome each and every one with genuine unconditional love. Without love, all the strategies in the world will never work.

People crave affection and connection. Show families that you understand their situation and love them anyway. Build your ministry around loving and caring for each family you meet. Just as Jesus would have done, welcome every skin color, every special need, every background, every financial status, and every situation with love. Teach them passionately. You never know if you are the first person to not make them feel worthless, unloved, and unwanted. Instead, make them feel welcome, valued, and worthy. Lead with love, and everything else will come with hard work, time, and intentionality.

Chapter 7

X-RAYS AND OREOS:HELP PARENTS LEAD THEIR CHILD TO CHRIST

BY TRISH WEEKS

O H, WHEN I WANT THEM TO KNOW about anything like *that,* I take them to the experts." I'll never forget the day I heard this from a parent. It was during a conversation about the parent talking to their child about God and how inadequate they felt. It was at this point that I realized I was failing. And it was a wake-up call to make some intentional changes in the way I saw and did ministry.

I'm not sure there are any "experts" on God. Sure, some people go to Bible colleges, do in-depth Bible studies, or use concordances and commentaries to dig deeper, but expert? I don't think so. And I didn't get the idea that this parent was lazy or didn't want to take the time to have this discussion with their child. They truly simply felt ill-equipped.

To be honest, at first the comment made me feel a little proud. I've been doing this for years and, of course, I think I'm pretty good at it. It has taken experience and practice (trial and error) to take a big truth and break it down for little minds and hearts to grasp. And let's be frank, kids' pastors don't always get a lot of compliments or recognition. So yeah ... a part of me was happy to hear it.

But another part of me screamed, "Wait, what? I barely know your kid." That's when I decided that I wanted to find a way to partner with parents in the spiritual growth of their children, not replace them as a spiritual authority.

God designed the family to be the primary spiritual influence. Deuteronomy instructs the Israelites to teach their children about God and His commands: *"Make sure your children learn them. Talk about them when you are at home. Talk about them when you walk along the road. Speak about them when you go to bed. And speak about them when you get up."* Deut. 6:7 (NIRV). The NLT phrases it: *"Repeat them again and again to your children."*

I laugh when I read verse 20 in *The Message: "The next time your child asks you, 'What do these requirements and regulations and rules that GOD, our God, has commanded mean?'"* Anybody who knows anything about kids knows they're going to ask questions. Deuteronomy 6 continues with God telling us how to answer them: tell them a story; tell them *your* story; share *your* experiences; tell them what I did for *you* and *your* family; tell them about the relationship I have with *you*.

This is where it gets sticky. Somewhere along the way, however unintentional, we have contributed to the falsehood that "we" can do it better. So, the question is, what can we do to help change that? How do we help parents feel success-ful, equipped, and empowered to be the spiritual authority in their family?

BAPTISM CLASS—EQUIPPING PARENTS

The first change I made was in a class I taught as the chil-dren's pastor. It was a baptism class for kids and parents. I'd been teaching it for several years and had gotten it down well. Kids were responding and parents commented that they re-ally learned a lot. They went on to say that I had explained it very well in a way they had never heard before, using object lessons and analogies the kids could relate to. But I realized just having the parents in the class wasn't really developing our mission statement of "Partnering with Families to Con-nect Kids to Christ."

I decided to try the proverbial: I do, you watch. I do, you help. You do, I help. You do, I watch. Jesus used this method with His disciples. He knew He wouldn't be around forever in bodi-ly form so He taught them how to teach. And He was an expert. So, I guess experts teach others how to teach others.

It was pretty easy, actually. I just tweaked the format to in-tentionally engage the parents in the discussion. I still did the primary teaching. I still used the kid-friendly object lesson and analogy. And then ... I asked them to lead the conversa-tion with their child right then. I gave each family a handout with some questions to direct the discussion. I had already answered the questions in my lesson; it was to reinforce what I had taught. I provided in parenthesis answers of what they should expect from their child in case they needed reassur-ance or if they felt biblically illiterate. I also had some of my kidmin leaders available to assist if they had any questions.

This was a big win in many ways. I was discipling the parents, but also discipling my leaders. It provided tools for parents to begin conversations about spiritual things if they hadn't already begun to initiate it at home, and it gave my leaders opportunity and experience to develop in their leadership. Overall, it provided a forum to *"equip the saints for the work of the ministry"* Eph. 4:12 (ESV) and *"entrust to reliable people who will also be qualified to teach others"* 2 Tim. 2:2 (NIV). Now I was starting to feel like an expert.

The following is a copy of the outline, lesson, and handout. I know I'll continually evaluate, improve, and probably totally re-write this discipling tool. A lot of it isn't original or revolutionary. It's a work in progress. But I do pray that it will be useful to you as a guide to help equip and empower parents.

BREAKDOWN OF THE LESSON

Origami

1. Use an origami object lesson to begin. Fold the paper into a house shape and talk about our homes. Ask them where God lives. (heaven)

2. Fold the house into an airplane and ask them if we can get to heaven in an airplane. (No!)

3. Continue folding and tearing part of it to look like a rocket ship and ask if we can get to heaven in a rocket ship. (No!)

4. Unfold it, and it's now in the shape of a cross. (The ONLY way we get to heaven is because we accept what Jesus did on the cross for our sins.)

X-Ray

Next, I show an x-ray of my son's hand. I ask what it's a picture of.

I ask if it's a picture of the inside or the outside of a hand. I explain that salvation is something that happens on the inside of us, in our hearts. I go over the ABCs of salvation (Admit, Believe, Confess), and then I provide the following questions in a handout to discuss in their family groups.

1. Review the x-ray illustration. (It represents salvation—what has happened on the inside.)

2. Review the ABCs

   a. Admit that you are a sinner (Romans 3:23)

   b. Believe that Jesus is God's Son (John 3:16; John 14:6)

   c. Confess that Jesus is Lord (Romans 10:9-10)

3. Ask your child:

   a. What is sin? (things we do wrong)

   b. Have you ever sinned? (*Be careful with this one. Sometimes the kids think we've teamed up to make them confess something to their parents ... lol.*)

   c. What is the problem with sin? (It separates us from God.)

   d. Who is Jesus? (God's Son)

   e. What did Jesus do for us? (died on the cross to pay for our sin; made a way for us to be right with God)

   f. What happens when you believe and trust in Jesus? (Our sins are forgiven, we receive eternal life, and will live with God forever.)

   g. Have you made Jesus the Lord of your life? OR, Do you trust Jesus with your whole life and believe that He died for you?

4. If they have, great! They're ready for the next step. If they have not, but you think they understand the ABCs and want to make Jesus Lord of their life, you can pray together right now.

Dear Heavenly Father, I admit that I have done things that are wrong and my sin should separate me from You forever. I believe that Jesus is Your Son and that He died for my sin. I accept His death as payment for my sin and confess that Jesus is my Lord and Savior. Thank you for loving me and giving me the gift of salvation and eternal life with You forever. Jesus, come into my heart and into my life and help me follow You all the days of my life. In Jesus Name, Amen.

REMEMBER: You are not saved by saying a prayer; you are saved by putting your faith in Christ as your Savior. Prayer is simply a way of expressing your trust in Christ for all He has done.

JESUS' TEAM

Since this is a baptism class, we take it further than the salvation discussion. I use a football jersey as an illustration. I remind them about the x-ray and of salvation being something that happens on the inside. I talk about the jersey and ask if they play sports and if they have a jersey. People wear jerseys to let others know which team they play on or who they are rooting for. Baptism is like this jersey; it lets others know you're on Jesus' team! I talk about baptism being a symbol of the death, burial, and resurrection of Jesus. Then we go back to groups with these questions.

1. Review the jersey illustration. (It's a way to show everyone that I'm on Jesus' team! It's an outward picture of what happened on the inside.)

2. Ask your child:

   a. Why should you get baptized? (because Jesus did and He told us to)

   b. What does it show everyone? (that I'm on Jesus' team; that I've decided to follow Jesus)

   c. What does going under the water and coming back up represent? (Jesus death, burial, and resurrection, and that I choose to leave my old life for a new one)

   d. Are you ready to get baptized?

OREOS

At the conclusion, each kid gets an Oreo and a small glass of milk and we "baptize" the Oreo! Lots of fun and yummy! We give them instructions for the baptism which will be the following week and send them home with a lesson they complete together. They return this for a prize to further reinforce the lesson.

THE 4/14 WINDOW

I would be preaching to the choir to state the importance of kids being saved at an early age. In fact, a phrase has been coined for this ideology: the 4/14 Window. An International Bible Society survey found 83% of all Christians make commitments to Jesus Christ between the ages of 4 and 14. Therefore, the "why" seems obvious to us as kidmin leaders, but what about the "how"? How do we engage and equip parents and families in today's world?

PRIORITIES

Sometimes we expend a lot of effort trying to get people to change their lifestyles—to make church a priority. Families might not choose to stop something else to make church a priority, but that doesn't mean they don't care. I read somewhere that non-Christians don't make a conscious decision to not come to church; they honestly just don't even think about it, in much the same way that you or I don't go to a synagogue on a Saturday. (When is the last time you said to your family, "Should we go to synagogue today or not?")

Christianity has never been about what we should do; it is about what Jesus did. Therefore, I encourage you to just be authentic, intentional, and available wherever you are. Most of the encounters people had with Jesus in the Bible were because of proximity. He ministered to those around Him and more kept showing up! As we begin to better equip our families (including kids!) to share the Gospel, their lives will be a beacon, drawing others to Jesus.

Let us not be like the leaders in Joshua's day as recorded in Judges 2:10 (The Message). *"Eventually that entire generation died and was buried. Then another generation grew up that didn't know anything of God or the work He had done for Israel."* Instead, let's help parents learn how to make it a priority in their family and have their own story to share as encouraged in Joel 1:3 (NLT). *"Tell your children about it in the years to come, and let your children tell their children. Pass the story down from generation to generation."*

Chapter 8

FAMILIES SERVING TOGETHER

BY MICHELLE BOWEN

RAKING LEAVES, FOLDING BULLETINS, packing lunches, stuffing envelopes, directing parking lot traffic, visiting homebound members, feeding the homeless, event-based ministry, praying over families, leading worship, teaching Bible lessons ... the list of ministry needs to be filled at any local church is extensive. Rarely do we lack opportunities where families can minister.

Yet, only 20% of the people seem to do 80% of the work in a church. This is the same across denominations and across the ocean. When a service opportunity comes across the horizon, how should it be communicated? Flyers and email seldom stir families to action. Personal communication is obviously better, but who should be asked? The mom with little ones at home would need child care. The family with teens is busy with sports and part-time jobs. Just when is it a good time to serve? If there were more room in the budget, we could hire someone. Maybe this project isn't that important. Perhaps, the service opportunity gets sidelined for now.

Yet, why do we serve at all? Why should people take time out of their busy lives to serve someone else? The answer is: Because it's scriptural! Serving is an act of obedience to God. It is a response of worship to Him.

Joshua 22:5 *"Love the LORD your God, and ... walk in all his ways ... keep his commandments ... cling to him and serve him with all your heart and with all your soul"* (ESV).

Galatians 5:13, *"but through love serve one another"* (ESV).

Not only are we called to serve, but we are to serve with all our hearts, all our souls, and to serve one another in love. Our obedience to the command to serve is not out of obligation, but out of worship. Our attitude toward how we give our time is just as important as the service we give.

Service is an act of worship. It is the worship that extends beyond Sunday morning singing, or Wednesday night prayer meetings. It is worship that goes beyond reading and reflecting upon your Bible. It's not that those things are not worship, they are in every essence of the word. Praising God and meditating on His Word is fulfilling the command of God and glorifying His Name. However, those expressions of worship are inward, an aspect of our personal relationship with God. Yet, we are to worship the Lord both inwardly and outwardly. Worshipping through serving Him points others to Him. God saved us with the intention that we would worship Him with good works.

Ephesians 2:8-10 (ESV), *"For by grace you have been saved through faith. And this is not your own doing; it is the gift of God, not a result of works, so that no one may boast. For we are his workmanship, created in Christ Jesus for good works, which God prepared beforehand, that we should walk in them."*

As an act of worship, our service should not be ritualistic, or performed as in paying a debt, but again, it should be from our hearts, from our souls, an expression of love. *"God loves a cheerful giver"* 2 Corinthians 9:7 (ESV).

In fact, Jesus says that the world will recognize us by our outward expression of love, by not only the deeds we do, but by the love we demonstrate as we serve. John 13:35 (ESV), *"By this all people will know that you are my disciples, if you have love for one another."*

This brings us to why families should serve together, and why it is important as ministry leaders to equip those families for service together. It's about discipleship. Throughout Scripture, we see families serving together. Fathers taught sons, and mothers taught daughters. The tribe (family) of Levites served as families in the temple before the Lord. When the walls of Jerusalem fell, Nehemiah organized the people by family, and they worked together serving the Lord.

Deuteronomy 6 tells us that we are to teach our children as we rise up, as we lay down, and as we walk along the way. In Psalm 78, we are told to proclaim to our children the wondrous things the Lord God has done. This is discipleship. It is only natural to speak of the things of the Lord while serving the Lord.

Most believers would agree that it's good to share the Gospel, to proclaim the wondrous deeds of our Father God, to share about the encouragement and comfort from the Holy Spirt. Rarely would anyone contend that discipleship is not important, nor would any argue against parents leading their children to follow Jesus. Yet, the statistics are still true. Twenty percent of the people do 80% of the work. How do we equip families to serve together? How have others accomplished this goal?

In our family, we have chosen that discipling our children comes before any other ministry. Yet, discipling our children requires service in ministry beyond our children. We have chosen to serve the Lord, together, as a family. Further, as a means to equip other families in this discipleship experience, we have nearly always invited others along the way. This seems to be the order of things in Scripture as well. Discipleship is living life together. Mark 3:14 (ESV), *"And he appointed twelve (whom he also named apostles) so that they might be with him and he might send them out to preach."*

Jesus didn't call the disciples to come to a meeting or a training event. He did have specific times of teaching with them, but they were with Him in His presence as He served the Father. He modeled for them, and then He sent them to do that same work.

We can do that, too! How do you know what ministry opportunities are available for families in your church? As a missionary, we are often asked, "What kind of mission can I take my families to experience?" As a member of several kid, youth, and family ministry groups on Facebook, I frequently see posts that ask where a team can go, or what kit can they buy to teach missions and ministry for their families. May I encourage you that lifelong discipleship will have a greater impact than any trip you take or kit you buy. They have their place, and they are worthy. What I am suggesting is that you consider how you can align with the ministries already present in your church and equip your families for discipleship while serving in those ministries.

We are missionaries, and our children have spent a great deal of time working on missions projects that are simply part and parcel to our lives. We wanted to give our children an opportunity to serve that was less connected to our immediate ministry. After praying for God's guidance, an opportunity arose for a volunteer custodian at our church. Our family spent a year cleaning toilets, sweeping floors, and washing windows on Thursday nights. In the beginning of that year, it took a couple of hours to get all the work done because either my husband or I supervised each task. We modeled, and we watched. In the beginning, the little ones spent more time pretending to clean, or got distracted by all the cool things (toys in the nursey, dry erase boards in Sunday school classrooms, or balls in the gym—even the water fountain was a delight). Yet, as time progressed, the older children learned to do certain tasks on their own, and the distractions lost some of their appeal for the little ones.

After six weeks, the older three (then 8, 10, and 12) were able to vacuum, sweep, and wash windows without supervision. Therefore, my husband and I could complete a task in the same room while they completed those tasks on their own. HOWEVER, this is not what we did. Seeing this as an opportunity for discipleship, we turned these simple tasks into an opportunity to develop leadership skills. The older three children were then charged with teaching those skills to their 4- and 6-year-old brothers. They were to train them to complete the task, and also to inspect the results of the task for completeness. We equipped them with encouraging and gentle words. We reminded them of what we did and what we said when we demonstrated the work.

Believe it or not, this was not a smooth transition. The little guys wanted to make everything into a toy. The dust mop was a May-pole. The rag was a puppet. They made nose prints on the glass windows and doors they just washed. This was frustrating for our older children. Yet, we did not abandon the older children to supervising the younger ones while we worked in another room. We were there, present, but watching. We gave reminders to the little ones about why we were doing the task at hand. We gave words of affirmation and direction to the older children. After a few more months, it took us only an hour to clean the entire building. Very little direction was necessary because we had a system, and everyone worked as part of a team.

Cleaning the building wasn't about the task though. This wasn't the main goal for our family. Working together, serving the Lord was the main objective. We were able to worship Him through our hands. We were able to develop leadership skills in our older children. As the tasks became routine, we were able to have conversations about life, and about the Lord. We played praise music and sang as we twirled brooms and swiped cloths. We experienced relational discipleship.

Last week, I had the pleasure of being audience to our 14-year-old daughter standing before over 100 people who had come out in support of the youth ministry at our church. She shared part of her testimony regarding spiritual growth in her life as a result of that ministry. I may be biased, but I believe our daughter is a deep thinker, and well spoken. However, she is shy. Ordinarily, speaking in front of a group much, much smaller would be uncomfortable. Yet, when she was asked to give her testimony, we had a conversation about the task. First, it was easy to discuss the situation because we have developed an open relationship as we spent time together. It is a natural progress of spending quality time together. Secondly, she was able to trust my advice as she had seen her father and I guide others in ministry her entire life.

Her concern was standing in the presence of so many people and speaking to them. She didn't want that attention, and it was immobilizing. Many can relate to that feeling. I told her that I completely understood. "How could you? You speak at conferences with more than 500 in attendance." True, I do. However, I was able to encourage her that when Daddy or I speak in front of all those people, it is not my role to entertain them, or to make them like me in anyway. Our role in all things is to reflect God's glory. 1 John 4:14 (ESV), *"And we have seen and testify that the Father has sent his Son to be the Savior of the world."* Colossians 3:23 (ESV), *"Whatever you do, work heartily, as for the Lord and not for men."*

When she stood before the crowd, and clearly shared what the Lord did in her life, she was able to do it with confidence because she understood that her actions led others to worship and glorify God in response.

Our family has also had the opportunity to be part of international missions even before my husband and I had ever traveled overseas in our current work. We collected and packed suitcases for those on the team. Even our 4-year-old was able to fold wash cloths and stuff toothbrushes into baggies.

Another family we know—Chris, Amber, and their children—manages a benevolence ministry at church. Every month, they sort clothes by size and gender for a big give-away at the end of the year.

At the same church, Brandon and Danielle oversee a community connection ministry feeding local families on Wednesday nights. These two families shop for and prepare food, set up tables and chairs, welcome and encourage both friends and strangers, and then clean up at the end of the night. They also invite other families to join them in the work. In this way, not only are they ministering to the community while discipling their own children, they are empowering other families to do the same.

In our ministry, we have coordinated conferences that included packets for each participant. We invite families to our home and children fill baggies with pins, pens, and candy, staple those baggies to the inside of a folder, and stuff the folder with the conference book and other printed material. At the end, we pray over those folders asking for God to encourage the workers in attendance and to bless the ministries of those churches for His glory.

We have also joined in at church, stuffing mercy bags for the homeless (2 bottles of water, 2 protein bars, a list of resource agencies in the area, a Gospel tract, and a one-day bus ticket pass), or for the police (protein and shelf-stable snacks, water, wet wipes). We have signed up to serve at the welcome desk at connection events such as our Car Show. Our family has also served as part of the clean-up crew after our Community Thanksgiving meal.

Another dear family—Tim and Noreen and their daughters—have served alongside us at a Bible camp for several years.

They have cleaned cabins, counseled campers, led teams, and various other things. When their daughter, Samantha, graduated from high school, she moved to camp and served there for two years as a missionary!

What are the ministries currently at your church? How can the families in your church serve alongside? Are there ways families can minister to the saints in your church? Can they serve those who are serving in leadership? Maybe a family with toddlers can make a meal for another family who is overseeing a large event. Perhaps a family with school agers and teens can rake leaves for the elderly members of the congregation.

How do you develop a ministry equipping families to serve the Lord together? Create a list of ministries within the church where families can serve and support in alignment with the mission of your church. Then, cast vision for the parents on why they should serve together. It is more than to complete projects and check items off a list. Serving together is an eternal investment of discipleship.

Chapter 9

UTILIZE MILESTONES

BY DANA WILLIAMS

WHETHER A SLEEP-DEPRIVED NEWBORN'S parent or a high school parent desperate to steer their teen back onto a right path, and everything in between, you've probably looked into parents' eyes as they've confessed they simply don't know how to raise kids. They say in desperation, "Kids don't come with an instruction manual." And we kind of wish they did!

But, maybe you can take a bit of comfort from the fact that you can't write a manual for raising children, because every kid is uniquely made in the image of God and every context for every kid is a little bit different. That means there isn't one exact path to bringing up young people who love Jesus and live for Him.

It's less like a trip on an interstate highway and more like an adventure through the wilderness. Generations before us have traveled this way and left some markers of parenting wisdom on the trails. As leaders of families in the local church, we act as guides for the heroes of this story: parents. Parents are the ones who have been admonished to *"Start children off on the way they should go and even when they are old they will not turn from it"* Proverbs 22:6 (NIV). With those who trust you to help guide them, your role is to lead them through this wilderness and point out where God already is all along the way.

ELEVATE COMMON MILESTONES

As a child grows, there are some fairly predictable landmarks along the path. Many families will stop and celebrate these milestones whether or not they're connected to your ministry. Just like an adventurer will stop to take in the summit view or pause and marvel at a geyser, parents are going to experience some wonder when they bring home their baby, send him off to kindergarten, notice (and panic) at his first crush, and cry at his graduation. As a leader, you can serve families by helping them infuse these experiences with an awareness and alignment to God.

BRINGING HOME BABY

Families are built through birth, adoption, and marriage, as well as other means. When a child joins a family, there is always a shift in the family dynamic. It's a milestone. Take note of the culture of your community. When a baby is born, do you mark the milestone with a baby shower or some other celebration? Do you also celebrate when a child is adopted? (Keep in mind that there is loss with every adoption, so seek out mentors and safe people who can help you lead well.) When a blended family is formed through marriage, it can be met with an array of emotions. I grew up in two blended families. I wonder what it might have been like to have ministry leaders walk beside my parents and me through that time pointing us to God's hand in our lives. No matter how a family is built, these moments will usually be marked with photos, relatives, friends, and gifts. As a ministry leader, you can and should point families back to God in these moments.

One of my favorite ways to do this is by giving a blessing, either from us or from another significant person. In Luke 1, we see Mary's cousin, Elizabeth, bless her and her baby, who is the Messiah. When Isaac was born, Sarah spoke over him that God brought her laughter and how others would laugh with her about what God had done in her life with Abraham. When King David brought Jonathan's son, Mephibosheth, into his home, he blessed him. A blessing gives us the opportunity to affirm who they are, how God is working in their lives, and what we hope for them. It's a chance for us to circle up with their people and speak life over their growing family!

BACK TO SCHOOL

Each fall, a parade of kid photos fills my social media feeds as kids head back to school. Parents marvel at how fast they're growing and beg time to slow down. In the church, you're marking the occasion by promoting class rosters and moving kids from one area of ministry to the next. These moments can easily pass by without much intention. Leaders can help guide parents through transitions between ministries with intentional rite of passage type events. A rite of passage event is pretty flexible and can be tailored to various contexts. It serves to help families widen the circle of godly influence on their child. Team-building activities are a powerful way to help kids connect with the older kids and new area of ministry.

It's also a perfect stopping point to equip parents for the next phase, giving them tools of what to expect in their child physically, mentally, emotionally, socially, and spiritually. It's a chance to get parents into a room while their kids are making connections with volunteers and other kids. You can not only equip parents with knowledge but offer them a tribe of others going through the same phase. Point out their fellow "adventurers," because they're a good resource and support to each other. They can help one another navigate the media and events their kids will encounter.

HAPPY BIRTHDAY TO YOU

In our home, we mark birthdays very literally with a new dash on the growth chart. It's fun to track the upward progress over time. We marveled at the six-inch growth spurt during my son's freshmen year of high school! What would it look like to take a moment to mark the spiritual growth of our kids through something as simple as a birthday card from one of their leaders? Imagine the impact of a whole series of cards that carried words like, "I watched your faith grow this year when you ...", "You're becoming more like Jesus! I see Him through your ..." "God says you are ... It's been fun to watch you realize it this year!"

POMP AND CIRCUMSTANCE

At some point, most parents will launch their kids into adult life. High school graduation is often the symbol of this milestone. Regardless of how you celebrate this event, which is both an ending and a beginning, you can point out God's presence through it. It's a natural point to trace the path you've traveled as you review the memories, photos, and videos. You can prompt parents to recall how God led and revealed Himself through those times. You can challenge them to pass along their stories. It's a terrific time for young adults to receive a blessing from parents or church leaders.

Once young adults are launched, parents find themselves in an unfamiliar place. They've spent years raising a child, and all-too-quickly it's over. For some, this is exciting and for others, it's devastating. Either way, these parents know the path first-hand and might find new purpose as a great encouragement to parents who are still in the thick of things. Seek out ways to give them opportunities to share their wisdom and help mark the trail for others.

"WOW, GOD!" MOMENTS

Just like adventurers hope to catch a glorious sunset sky, a glimpse of wildlife, or a trail of a shooting star, along the path there are also some milestones that are unpredictable. You hope and pray you have the opportunity to see the wonder of God at work in the life of a child. When you do, you can guide parents to pass through these moments as more than just going through the spiritual motions. These are opportunities to leave behind a marker on the path of their child's life.

CHILD DEDICATION

Child dedication is a commitment to establish a partnership between family and church to have a positive influence on the spiritual development of a child. As a leader, you can challenge parents to consider the end game. What do they want it to look like when this little one is ready to launch? You can ask them to widen the circle and invite others in to help them through the process of raising up kids who are for God and for neighbor. We exhort them to create daily and weekly rhythms in their family that point them back to God. In our child dedication, we give gifts that remind them to be intentional with the weeks they have raising that child. We ask them to appoint friends or family as *paidagogos*. These are people who will come alongside parents and help them shape their child's faith. As the family stands to make their commitment statement, the paidagogos join them as a symbol of their commitment to help promote spiritual development.

GREETINGS FROM CAMP!

Being entrusted with a person's child is a significant matter. We live in a frightening world, so if a parent sends their child to a sleep-away camp, it's a big deal. It compels you to make the most of the break from the routines of home and church. Most leaders and parents agree that a lot of growth can take place at camp! That's why family and church invests so much in creating camping opportunities for children and students.

You can help parents set a tone of both fun and growth for their camper by asking them to write a letter to their child about what they hope for their child's week at camp. Collect the letters ahead of time and have kids' ministry leaders fill in any letters that are missing. Campers receive their letters when they arrive at camp. It leaves an intentional mark on the path where they might otherwise only bring back a suitcase full of dirty clothes ... assuming they actually changed clothes and bathed at some point during the week!

You can also serve families by helping to connect them to another person to pray over the child while she is away at camp. We create a wristband with every child's name and make them available to those who would commit to pray for that specific child while they're at camp. Kids know that there is someone at home praying for them by name. At the end of camp, kids get a notecard and are asked to write a note to the person who prayed for them about their camp experience.

IT'S A FAMILY THING

In your role as a guide to parents, you need to intentionally look for ways to engage parents as the spiritual leaders of their child in ministry programming. Create space for the family to experience God together.

The holiday celebrations you design can offer parents the chance to lead. We hosted an event where families could imagine themselves back in time on the streets of Bethlehem on the night of Jesus' birth. Parents walked with kids from tent to tent, where they experienced the excitement of a baby born in a stable. Parents entered into the story and helped their kids create mementoes of the night. Provide them with a Bible countdown or advent to turn their attention to God during holiday seasons.

Send them on a scavenger hunt together where they work together to solve clues from scripture.

Offer a worship service designed for parents and kids together. Whether a ministry can do it once a quarter, once a month, or every week, the experience sets up parents to be able to start spiritual conversations with their kids from a shared memory together.

TODAY IS THE DAY

Everything hinges on the Gospel. Faith in Christ alone saves us and changes us. Jesus' work draws us near to God and sends us out for Him. So, you ought to equip parents with resources that help them share their own faith with their child and the words that help them talk about the Gospel.

When you get the opportunity to see a child in your ministry trust in Christ, there's always celebration in God's Kingdom. You can partner with parents in bringing that celebration into their home and the local church by taking the time to recognize when a child trusts Jesus through gifts, words, or a special observance.

BAPTISM

When a child trusts in Jesus for salvation, a first step for their new life of faith is to obey Christ's example of baptism. Leading up to that choice, as a ministry we provide materials or a parent/child class about baptism. When a child in our ministry chooses to take this step of faith, it's another cause for celebration and reflection. We create a video featuring the child or student and their statement of faith. It's pretty amazing to live in a time where we can easily capture that moment in time and keep a record of it! We also like to come alongside parents by giving a gift that helps a child begin to take more ownership of their spiritual growth, like a devotional book that introduces ways to grow in faith.

SEND ME

As children get older, they'll encounter more opportunities to serve. Partner with parents to help students discover their gifts and their interests. They may want to serve in the local church, in the community, or in the world. They may also need a nudge in that direction. Look for ways to affirm a child's faith and create opportunities for him to discover how God might have him serve. Give parents resources about spiritual gifts to create conversations around that. Give them common words to talk about it. We like to use Jesus' example as our Prophet, Priest, and King to describe ways God's people are gifted. Set up opportunities for kids and parents to try out different ministries together. Look for ways to create a positive feedback loop between parents and kids about areas of giftedness and service. Send them out and pray over them often. Part of launching kids is commissioning them to a life for God and for neighbor.

As you lead parents through this crazy adventure of raising kids, you don't have to have the manual that answers every parenting dilemma. You'll never have all the answers and the scenery of culture, media, and challenges changes daily. What you can offer as a guide is to help them become more aware of God and more aligned with Him as they take in the milestones along the way. They're probably going to experience adding a new family member, birthdays, and school years launching, so as leaders and guides you can lead them to see the mystery of God in it all. You get to guide families and children to and through their own steps of faith. It's naturally easier to see God in these moments. As a leader, you can help mark the trail at each step with gifts, words ,and experiences that help both parents and kids remember their journey of faith.

Chapter 10

GRANDPALS

BY HOLLY ROE

MANY CHURCHES, ESPECIALLY THOSE with smaller congregations, struggle with volunteer recruitment. After years as a leader in children's ministry on staff at small and large churches, I've been privileged enough to make mistakes that have led to valuable lessons. I hope these lessons will help other ministry leaders as they seek to avoid the hidden "landmines" of ministry.

Part of my job today is to help show children's ministry leaders where these potential explosive issues lie before they encounter them and have them blow up in their faces. I've compiled a list of those potential landmines, and one of the top items on that list is the issue of recruiting volunteers from the wrong places. I know what it's like to be at a smaller church and not have a large selection when it comes to volunteers. I also know what it's like to serve at a very large church and have to weed through an excessive number of potential volunteers, as well. One truth that I've found in all churches, large and small, is that we have a tendency to recruit most of our volunteers for children's ministry from the busiest generation—the adults who have children participating in the ministry.

I've even heard of churches requiring parents and guardians to serve time in the nursery or children's ministry department out of obligation. Because they have children who are participating in those ministry programs, leaders present the volunteer positions to parents as a requirement. These parents are made to feel like they need to do their duty and serve since their children are the beneficiaries. This may seem like a good idea and an easy way to fill spots; however, I believe this is a potential landmine that can blow up if you aren't careful.

Some parents or guardians may not be believers or may be new believers. They may not have grown up in church or even know the basic Bible stories. They may not be ready or equipped with the gifts or skills to teach their own children, and certainly not other people's children. Some could be in life situations in which they are in need of discipleship just as much as, if not more than, their own children. Many parents with younger children work full time, some are stay-at-home parents, or they might be grandparents raising their grandchildren. Some have children all day because they homeschool or are educators in a school system. They are busy at the office, are running back and forth between ball fields and dance practice, concerts, and school functions, and are living in the busiest seasons of their lives. Requirements that apply to every parent or guardian could compromise the value and integrity of your ministry and can rob some congregants of the opportunity to gain discipleship training or attend worship when they really need to be part of it!

Gravitating toward the busiest generation and expecting the most commitment and time from them as children's ministry leaders can be detrimental to your ministry if you aren't careful. When it comes to serving in children's ministry, quite often the busy ones are our go-to group!

Just because someone has children does not mean they're good at working with children in ministry. Young parents are sometimes in dire need of fellowship, discipleship, training, and worship with other believers who will help support and train them to be spiritual leaders to their children. Obviously, there are situations in which you'll encounter people who have a strong desire to be in the children's ministry department as a volunteer. They're always present, and as long as they are also participating in worship and discipleship at other times during the week, it occasionally works. But we must watch carefully, because even the best and most gifted children's ministry leaders can burn out if we allow them to work and never refuel. No one can keep going on an empty tank. Eventually, they stall and start to putter to a halt. To prevent this, we must be very strategic when we schedule our leaders. Schedule wisely, thoughtfully, and not too frequently.

Many of the wisest people I've encountered on my spiritual journey are older folks who have experienced a lot of life, have made more mistakes, and have had more time to study the Scripture. Even those who may not have begun their walk with Christ until later in life have learned life lessons the hard way before Christ and can testify to the powerful things He has brought them through. If we aren't considering the older generations when recruiting for children's ministry leadership, we're missing out on some of the best and wisest leadership potential.

Thinking outside of the young and middle-aged landscape and expanding our volunteer search to include those a little further on the journey gives us a broader vision and takes in some people who have had a longer spiritual trek. Frequently, those with the longer journeys have more insight because they've covered a lot more ground, seen a lot more of the big picture, and had to navigate around many more roadblocks and wrecks than those in the early stages of their journeys. We can always benefit from the wisdom of someone who has been there already. There's value in that kind of wisdom, but sometimes we miss out on the depth of that when it comes to children's ministry. I believe this is due to a misconception that children are not capable of much more than learning basic Bible stories and that God loves them ... not that those things are not important, but they can do so much more than that!

God used children in mighty ways all throughout Scripture, and if you look closely you'll see that in many instances those children were led and mentored by great leaders who were like grandparents to them. God told Moses to groom Joshua (Exodus 17:9) and teach him how to write and keep records as he had learned in Pharaoh's school of government. He was grooming Joshua to take over and knew that only the wisdom from a very experienced leader would be sufficient for teaching the kind of knowledge necessary for Israel's next leader of this caliber. Moses was still mentoring and teaching Joshua even at the age of 120! He made mistakes along the way (Num. 20:12), and those mistakes undoubtedly gave Moses a testimony and the experience to prepare Joshua. Scripture tells us that after the death of Moses, *"Joshua the son of Nun was full of the spirit of wisdom, for Moses had laid his hands on him. So the people of Israel obeyed him and did as the Lord had commanded Moses"* Deut. 34:9 (NLT).

Giving ample opportunity for leaders who are a little further along in their journeys to continue to leave a legacy and speak into the next generations is something every leader should be intentional about. We must use every resource to equip and prepare our young people to run this race, and the more experienced runners are an invaluable resource to us all. As we reach out to hand off the Kingdom work of evangelism, our children will be reaching out to take the baton. What a shame if we have the opportunity to foster mentorship from every living generation ahead of them, but we only focus on the one closest to them. When we only focus on gaining leadership from one or two generations removed, we are robbing our children of wisdom that is sometimes literally sitting right beside them in the next room.

Grandparents, whether biological or not, are often one of the top two influencers in a child's life. Some of your greatest recruitment efforts in children's ministry should be taking place with the older generations in your church. You will indeed have some amazing workers from the parents of your children, but we should also put forth some intentional effort to recruit from the older pool of congregants as well. This takes some thoughtfulness and strategy.

When we require or make people feel obligated to serve in certain areas, we end up with half-hearted efforts from people with a lack of commitment. This leads to unprepared teachers who are late or don't show up, more discipline issues with children, stress, frustration, and complaints. We never want anyone to serve the Lord, and especially not the littlest of His children, for any other reason than because they want to speak the Gospel into the next generation in order to build up the Kingdom of God! All leaders, whether young or seasoned, should serve out of a passion to win the next generation to Christ and equip them to do the ministry of the Lord. Our mandate as leaders in the church is laid out very clearly in Ephesians 4: *"And he gave the apostles, the prophets, the evangelists, the shepherds and teachers, to equip the saints for the work of ministry, for building up the body of Christ"* Eph. 4:11-12 (ESV).

Sometimes we have a misconception that our main job as leaders is to get people to come to church so they can hear the Gospel. Scripture, however, tells us that our main job is to "equip the saints" so they are the ones going outside the walls of the church each day and winning people to Christ! Our real job is to build the Church (capital C), not just to build the church (lowercase c). Obviously, if we are successful at equipping saints, church growth should be a by-product of the passion we are seeding into congregants. Attendance should increase due to people saying, "You have to come visit my church. It changed my life!" rather than, "You have to come visit my church. Our preacher is cool, my kids have fun, and we have a coffee bar!" I'm not saying it's a bad thing to have a cool preacher, have a blast with kids, and have a coffee bar, but if we fail to equip people to do the work of evangelism outside the walls of the church, we're building more of a country club than the divine Kingdom. The job of building up this Kingdom is not solely the responsibility of the younger and busiest generations. It's not just left to those who are one generation removed. All the generations of elders ahead of children are to raise up those children in the ways of the Lord.

PRACTICAL IDEAS

So how do we foster this helpful and necessary influence from older generations within a community of believers? Today's kids are not like the generation of kids our grandparents raised. Many older people say that the generations being raised today are less respectful and more difficult to teach. How can we create environments that encourage relationships that bridge this generation gap? The first realization we must have is that kids today *are* different. They do interact differently. They are exposed to more. They are more connected to the outside world. The digital age has expedited our children's exposure in every way. They can be harder to manage in classroom settings; they're sometimes sassy and rude! I bet the "eye roll" didn't happen a lot when my grandmother was a little girl.

Consider a tool I've used called "Grandpals." This is a ministry idea that was born out of a desire to help the older generation realize that they are not too old and they do have what it takes to serve in children's ministry. If an older person has a skill or trade that they can teach to the younger generation such as building a birdhouse, cooking a homemade spaghetti dinner, baking fresh cookies from scratch, canning apple butter, quilting, building a campfire, etc., then they can add their name to a list, and kids can sign up for these workshops. I never put more than ten kids in a group to keep them manageable. I also assign an older youth or adult helper for each group. You don't want to overwhelm anyone with too many children at once. I told my Grandpals to be prepared to not only teach their skill but also to share their faith stories as they taught. I told them to get to know the kids, ask questions, and build relationships.

Before Grandpals, the older generation didn't even know the names of the children in our church. After Grandpals, several things began happening. I saw a great bridge being built and a generation gap begin to close. People I would've never thought to ask were now willing to step up and start teaching Sunday school classes. Older people began to invest and became more aware of what children's ministry was doing to teach the next generation. Instead of disrespectful kids running over and ignoring older folks at church dinners, I saw kids carrying trays for their Grandpal buddies and I heard older people say things like, "Hi Johnny, how was your soccer game?" The older generation began to notice things about the children that they never noticed before, and the younger generation began to respect the older generation!

The relationships that were built set up an ideal situation for intergenerational ministry to begin. These relationships could be the key to a successful grooming and equipping of your little saints in the building of the Kingdom.

Chapter 11

FIRST IMPRESSIONS

BY JACK HENRY

MANY OF US WHO GO TO CHURCH, and have been going for a long time, have forgotten what it's like for a family to visit a church for the first time. I honestly believe we have to strive to remember that experience, and never forget it. Why? Because there are families going through this every week at our churches! Have you ever been to a church where it seemed very mechanical? You know what I mean. People shook your hand (if they even did that), and said, "Good to have ya," but there was no heart behind it?

Did you know that most families will make up their minds whether or not they're coming back to your church within the first 10 minutes? It's true! So that tells me that we need to get it right from the start. My dad told me many times when I was young, "Son, be careful when making a first impression, because you can never get it back." When parents see that family is a high priority for a church, they envision that church as a place where their family members can learn, worship, serve, and laugh together, helping them grow closer to God and closer to each other. In order for this to happen, please understand that it all starts on your ...

Website. Believe it or not, most people will go to your website before they come to your church. This being the case, I will boldly say that your website is an important part of your first impression ministry! This is where the sermon begins, so allow me to park and preach a little.

If your website is not attractive to visitors and engaging your members, you're not alone. Two out of three churches consider their websites to be "ineffective." That's bad news! But even worse news is: if your website's not working FOR your church, then it's actually working AGAINST it.

Fair or not, everything about your church's website reflects on your ministry. If your website is poorly organized, dull, unattractive, outdated, or incomplete, it creates the impression that your church also is disorganized, dull, dowdy, out of touch, or unable to communicate the most basic information—and who wants to go to a church like that? Whether your church actually is any of those things is beside the point; it's the impression you're making that counts. That first impression affects your church's ability to attract newcomers through its website.

This being said, we need to make sure our sites are up to date, user friendly, cool, and filled with vital information that families need to see. Visitors will listen to sermons, so hopefully you have video available for that. They will go to your ministry pages and search. If past events are still on the site, it looks bad. Amazing websites are not that expensive these days. Honestly, it's an investment you should make! If you feel that your church site is ineffective, then here are some fast fixes that will greatly help.

Your site should clearly communicate what makes your church unique. There is no one else in the world just like you, and there is no church like yours! The spiritual community you have is unique to all others around you. What unique promise does your church offer people? Answer that question and make sure it's your ministry's point of power on the web.

Your site should run on a secure connection. Google has changed the way websites are displayed in Chrome, and other companies are following Google's lead. As a result, visitors to your website may now see "Not secure" next to your website address, along with an alarming warning, such as, "Your connection to this site is not private. Information you submit could be viewed by others (like passwords, messages, credit cards)." To avoid the appearance that your ministry is compromising your website visitors' security, you now need a security certificate installed on your website.

Your site should tell the truth. What you put on your site creates expectations, which then must be fulfilled when new people walk in your doors. If you say on your site that you're a warm and loving place, and new people walk in expecting that (because we have created that expectation) but experience the opposite, then they'll begin to suspect that other things they read and saw are false, as well. Never promise anything you can't deliver!

Your site should welcome guests and answer key questions. Did you know that your church website serves two different, and yet equally important, audiences? It services people looking for a new church home and those who have already made your church their home. Studies have confirmed that 77% of those attending church less than three months said that the website was important in their decision to attend. Your website answers questions like: Where are you located? What time are services? How long does a service last? Do I need to dress up? What do you have for my children? Where can I park? When these and other questions are asked and answered in the "I'm New" page, you'll have a win.

Your site should be easy to navigate. Make sure visitors can see what's available on your site from any page, and be able to go there with just one click. Web users have very little patience for sites that are not well built and thought out.

Your site should be current and correct. When you read wrong information, what impression do you get? You know those churches that leave an event with date and time on the sign 2 months after the event is over? It looks just as ridiculous on the website.

Make sure your site provides complete information, is integrated with social networks people already use, provides free podcasts of Sunday services, is evolving, and is mobile friendly. To put it all in one phrase, "Your website should be a ministry in and of itself."

Parking Lot. First impressions are everything and it's one thing that's hard to fix if you blow it. You should have friendly people smiling and waving. At a friend's church in Georgia, their parking lot greeters wear different color gloves and funny hats. He's gotten tons of smiles and compliments from visitors about this. What can you do to spruce up your parking lot ministry? Do you even have one? If you answered "no," then you need to get one. And make sure these people love to smile and are genuinely happy when people pull in! Make sure as well that they are knowledgeable and would know what to say when someone stops, rolls down the window, and has a question.

You should have designated parking for guests, especially for families with babies and toddlers (making sure these spaces are close to the nursery area). And these spaces should be well marked. Be ready with umbrellas if it's raining. Leave something on their windshield. Maybe popcorn? With a note that says, "Thanks for popping in." What I'm saying is that the sermon begins on the website and flows into the parking lot. New families hear a lot of preaching long before they ever hear the pastor speak from the platform! If you don't do this right, then it makes it much harder on the family as they walk into the church.

Greeters. When people walk through your doors, what do they see? What do they hear? Do they see friendly faces that say, "We've been expecting you, and we're so glad you're here!" Or do they see faces that say, "Seriously? More new people? Ugh. Let me drag myself over there and help these poor souls." People know if you're genuine. *Again, we have to remind ourselves every week that families are usually nervous when coming to a church for the first time.* I am convinced that if we always remember that, then it will change the way we respond to these families. Yes, our greeters should be super friendly but also knowledgeable. They need to be trained in knowing where people go. Nursery goes there. Preschool is here. Elementary is there, and it's even better when there is someone to walk them to those areas and hand them off to even more amazing people who make the first time check-in a thing of beauty! Just make sure to have the right people in your first impressions ministry because it will make a huge impact on whether these guests return to your church.

After 35 years of trying and doing, I've found that it works best when there are happy people right there where the new families check in. Welcome the parents, yes. But make sure the kids are really welcomed. Get down on their level, make eye contact, and let them know how happy you are that they are there. This goes a long way!

We have greeters at the top of the steps as well. Then a few more at the entrance door of our Kidz Theatre. Make sure you have a good group of kids, from different ages, who serve as your key welcomers. It really makes a new child feel amazing and accepted when this happens. They should be walked to their class and never left to find their way alone. That will not set well with them or with parents.

Be ready to make new kids feel welcomed in your services. You can extend a special welcome when you let them come to the stage and spin a big wheel for prizes. They always get KIDZ KASH to spend at our store. Hey, they're kids right? Sometimes we forget that.

Clean and Cool Kids' Areas. Clutter and old boring colors will be your enemy. The inside and entrance to your kidmin areas should match what year it is outside. Make sure the signage is great, as well. It's disheartening to walk around a church not knowing where to go. You can never overdo signage. Music should be playing in the hallways. The atmosphere should be bright and fun and filled with excitement so the kids will want to stay and return. There are two questions the parents will ask their children when they get back in the car: Did you have fun? What did you learn? This will greatly determine whether or not the family will return. No kidding. Look around your areas. Take a good look. What can be changed? What can you throw out? A little paint can go a long way. This leads me to my last (but certainly not least) of my points.

Family Friendly Vision Begins with the Pastor. Let's face it folks, if the pastor and leadership do not have a family friendly vision, then it will be very difficult to get it all done right. That vision is obvious to families from the moment they make first contact with your church. Listen to me please, because I've been there! I was at a church that grew from 500 to 1500 in 4 years. We ran 400 in kids' church and 275 teens on Wednesdays. Why? Because the staff made sure it was a family friendly atmosphere. But we had to fight for it. It was hard. After a while the lead pastor decided to turn the ship around and go another direction. It did not matter what we did, people left. We begged and pleaded but to no avail. Loooooong story short ... a staff of 12 ended up leaving. Sadly, and it breaks my heart to even type this, that church now runs about 8 kids in children's ministry. Yes, I said 8. The pastor, after 12 years, recently contacted me asking for help. I'm now helping them get back on track. I tell ya, a big piece of my heart has always been there and it's a joy to be involved, even a little. Would you pray for them?

Let me end this by reminding you that new families are usually very nervous when visiting a church for the first time. I am convinced that if we remember that in all we do, then it will change the way we respond to these families. Let's do it right, because God expects it and families deserve it.

Chapter 12

HELP FOR HURTING FAMILIES

JOY CANUPP

NOT ONE OF US IS EXEMPT FROM DEALING with pain. Families all around us are hurting for a wide range of reasons. Some of those hurts are direct results of poor choices. Many of those hurts are life happenings that could not have been avoided. Regardless, as you strive to minister to these families, you need to have some great resources at your fingertips that you can access when you have a ministry opportunity.

When folks are hurting, they are tender, they want to not be in pain, they want answers. The fact is that painful situations often provide a unique ministry opportunity that you should be ready for. You don't have a magic wand (and you shouldn't pretend that you do), but you do have the hope found in Jesus as well as practical ways to come alongside and help these families.

It's a good point of reminder that crisis situations look very different in the eyes of adults and the eyes of children. Adults and teens in the family will have understanding of the overall gravity of the situation, long-term implications, and the process of recovery/healing that they need to walk through. Children will view the crisis as a crisis. Regardless of the specifics, children react to having their worlds turned upside down. They will not comprehend that recovery/healing is ahead. They'll only see the devastation and hurt of the day (sometimes of the moment). All of this will cause children to respond (or "act out") in a number of ways which will add additional work and pain for the parent(s). Remembering this up front, should challenge you to not only be prepared to address the specific cause of hurt for these families but also assist in any way you can with the various reactions of the child involved.

Let's help hurting families! This chapter aims to help you create or strengthen your knowledge base and your practical toolkit for extending a helping ministry hand.

Before moving into those areas, let's acknowledge the power of prayer. Prior to jumping to practical, let's cover each situation, each person, each word offered, each deed done, completely in prayer. Let's affirm that God loves these families more than we do, that He knows every single intricate detail of the hurtful situation past, present ,and future, and that He will guide you in the part He intends you to play in these precious lives.

Let's also acknowledge the power of a simple handwritten note. Regardless of the circumstance, taking time to write a note and share Scripture of hope and God's promises can go a long, long way in ministering to hurting families. That note will likely be placed in a Bible, on a dresser, or some other area where it is seen often. That note will likely be treasured for months and years to come.

Pray. Send a note. And, then ...

GENERAL PRACTICAL WAYS TO HELP

... be equipped to know next best steps! The most important way that you can equip yourself in this area is to be proactively and consistently adding to your toolkit. Always be on the lookout for great resources that you can fully trust and find confidence in and ones that agree with what your church teaches. These resources may come in the form of individuals, counselors, community groups, books, websites, or Facebook groups.

Rather than trying to retain them in your memory, decide on a way to document them for quick and easy access. When a family in need crosses your path, the last thing you need to do is go digging through a stack of papers or trust your mind to suggest a helpful resource.

Whether a manual filing system, Evernote files, Google Docs or some other format, choose a method and get it started. You can add topics as you go. You can fill in with resources as you come across them. But getting started is a huge step rather than putting it off until tomorrow.

In fact, why don't you pause reading for just a moment and think through which system might work for you. Decision made? What will you need to get it started? Need file folders and labels? Add them to your shopping list or put them in your Amazon cart. (Yes, right now!) Planning to create a notebook in Evernote? I'll wait while you set that up. Something else? Go ahead and take that first small step now.

Once you have the beginnings of your system, it's time to think through some of the endless ways that families may be hurting. The remainder of this chapter won't be exhaustive, but it will get you off to a great start.

General resources to add to your file

- *When Helping Hurts* (Corbett & Fikkert)

- *When Children Grieve: For Adults to Help Children Deal with Death, Divorce, Pet Loss, Moving, and Other Losses* by John W. James

- Stephen Ministry - stephenministries.org

- Hope 4 Hurting Kids (wide range of topics) - hope4hurtingkids.com/

- Living Free (groups, curriculum and resources for all ages) - livingfree.org/

- Contact information for local and trusted pediatricians, pediatric psychologists, and counselors

Ideas to add to your file

- A tutor. If a family is overcome with pain, the children may fall behind in their schoolwork. Take note of the situation and offer to connect them with a tutor, if appropriate.

- Meals. Again, if the pain is intense, practical things like hearty meals may fall by the wayside and the family may resort to fast food options. Consider setting up a meal schedule and getting others involved in that process. Meal Train (mealtrain.com/) and Sign Up Genius (signupgenius.com/) are two options to make that an easy online process that can be shared on Facebook and email.

- Basic Needs. There may not be time or energy for shopping. Does the family need a couple of bags of basic household supplies from Wal-Mart? You can make that happen for them!

- Depending on the age of the child(ren) and the situation, consider giving a stuffed animal, special pillow, or blanket as an extra means of comfort.

As you walk through various areas that cause pain within families, your goal (beyond prayer and a note of care) should be to connect these families to community and practical helps/resources. In each of the following areas, some of those are provided. Be sure to take time to transfer those from this book to your toolkit. You'll be glad you did!

DEATH AND GRIEF

Not if, but when ... families will cross paths and walk the grief journey. It's part of life. The relationship of the person who has died will give more specific indicators about how best to minister to this family. At minimum, send a personal card, give a hug, and consider taking a meal. For a child who has lost a close family member, consider purchasing a picture frame that can hold a special photo of that person. If you want to go a step further, you could do a bit of Facebook stalking (in a good way!) and try to find a picture to have printed to place in the frame before gifting it.

Equip yourself with a basic understanding of the grief process. Get a handle on the differences in the way adults and children grieve. Be prepared to talk with parents and equip them to walk the grief journey with their kids.

Resources to add to your file on death and grief

- The Stages of Grief - grief.com/the-five-stages-of-grief/
- GriefShare - griefshare.org/
- Video/Info About Grieving Children - griefshare.org/children
- KinderMourn - kindermourn.org/
- Hope 4 Hurting Kids Resources on Grief - hope4hurtingkids.com/grief/helping-children-deal-grief/
- *Someone I Love Died* by Christine Harder Tangvald (written for ages 4-8)

Consider offering a parent class on "Kids and Grief" to prepare moms, dads, and grandparents before they deal with a death in their personal world.

FINANCIAL STRESS

From job loss to major medical expense to mismanaging finances, financial stress can cause tremendous pain within a family. Knowing bits of the situation will help you determine the best route to go in terms of helping.

Resources to add to your file on financial stress

- Dave Ramsey's *Total Money Makeover*, Financial Peace (class) and/or personal connection with an ELP - daveramsey.com/
- Crown Financial Ministries - crown.org/
- Local food banks and organizations that help with utility bills
- Folks in your church family who enjoy anonymous giving when families are in financial crisis

MEDICAL OR SPECIAL NEED DIAGNOSIS

The news from the doctor was not good. The family is in shock. They are often scared and feel isolated. To let them know quickly that they are not walking this road alone is critical, and then to connect them with others will make a huge difference in their lives.

Resources to add to your file on medical diagnosis

- *How to Explain a Diagnosis to a Child: An Interactive Resource Guide for Parents and Professionals* by Janet Arnold and Francine McLeod
- "Explaining a Cancer Diagnosis to Your Child" - iscc-charity.org/explaining-a-cancer-diagnosis-to-your-child/
- Contact information for local support communities.

MARRIAGE/PARENTING/RELATIONSHIP ISSUES

Relationships are hard. Hard work. When families stop working on their relationships, often painful situations occur.

Whether it is spouse to spouse, parent to child, sibling to sibling or other combinations, there are various issues that may surface. Non-traditional family units will also have specific needs and sources of pain.

Resources to add to your file on marriage/parenting/relationships

- Focus On the Family - focusonthefamily.com/
- FamilyLife - familylife.com/
- Shaunti Feldhahn books - shaunti.com/
- Dr. Henry Cloud books - drcloud.com/
- Les and Leslie Parrott books - lesandleslie.com/
- Dr. Gary Chapman books - 5lovelanguages.com/

DIVORCE

Prior to a divorce, pain already existed. Many think that a divorce will make the pain disappear. But, in fact, the hurt often increases significantly for a time—especially for children (of all ages). There can be healing and new peace and new routine after a divorce but it takes time. It takes walking through the grief process. And, it takes (more) time.

Resources to add to your file on divorce

- DivorceCare - divorcecare.org/
- DivorceCare for Kids - dc4k.org/
- *Talking to Children About Divorce* by Jean McBride

ADOPTION CHALLENGES

The excitement and patience of parents in the adoption process is amazing. When the process is complete and the child is in his new forever home, much rejoicing takes place. Unfortunately, not all adoption processes have a happy ending. Some get interrupted and do not result in an adoption. Others are complete but the transition for the child and adoptive family is difficult.

Resources to add to your file on adoption

- Empowered to Connect (podcast, conference, huge resource library) - empoweredtoconnect.org/
- Trust Based Relational Intervention (find a TBRI practitioner in your area) - child.tcu.edu
- *The Connected Child: Bring Hope & Healing To Your Adoptive Family* by Purvis/Cross/Sunshine
- *Beyond Consequences, Logic, and Control: A Love-Based Approach to Helping Attachment-Challenged Children with Severe Behaviors* by Forbes/Post
- Tapestry Ministry - tapestryministry.org/
- Refresh Gatherings (conferences, retreats, camps) - refreshgatherings.org/

SUBSTANCE ABUSE

The pain experienced in a home where substances are being abused is often hidden for a long time. When it surfaces, it is likely coming from a critical and desperate situation.

Resources to add to your file on substance abuse

- Addiction Resource - addictionresource.com/
- "Effects of Parental Substance Abuse On Children And Families" - aaets.org/article230.htm
- Contact and meeting information for local recover groups

DOMESTIC VIOLENCE/ABUSE

As with substance abuse, the hurt and harm experienced in a home where abuse of a family member is happening often remains secretive. When it starts becoming public, layers of additional pain including embarrassment and anger will likely occur.

Resources to add to your file on domestic violence/abuse

- The National Domestic Violence Hotline - thehotline. org/
- "Children and Domestic Violence" - nctsn.org/content/ children-and-domestic-violence
- "Impact of Domestic Violence on Children and Youth" - nctsn.org/content/children-and-domestic-violence
- Contact information for local safe shelters and counselors who specialize in this area
- Be sure to know your state laws if you find yourself suspecting abuse in a situation that has not become public yet.

NATURAL DISASTERS

The surprise element of this type of pain for families makes the situation even tougher. And, depending on the disaster, you and the entire community may be affected. To have resources that you can tap into ahead of time is extra crucial.

Resources to add to your file on natural disasters

- Southern Baptist Disaster Relief - namb.net/send-relief/ disaster-relief/
- Your state's Baptist DR (easy to Google)
- Red Cross - redcross.org/
- Samaritan's Purse - samaritanspurse.org/what-we-do/ us-disaster-relief/

LOCAL, NATIONAL, AND WORLD OCCURRENCES

We should not overlook the things that happen in our world that end up on the news and overtaking social media. Kids hear far too much and when that happens they are forced to process things that their age level is not ready for. Parents spend too much time focused on the media and can almost become consumed with any given incident even when it does not affect them directly. Parents may experience deep levels of fear and be overwhelmed. It's the current world we live in. When tragedy strikes, kids and parents alike are trying to process the information, handle their emotions, and get questions answered. In ministry, we should be ready to step up and be part of that process with them. From mass shootings to airplanes flying into buildings, to sweeping forest fires, to leaders being called out and quickly removed for wrongdoings, to all that falls between, you can add things to your toolkit to minister to families who experience hurt from these occurrences.

Resources to add to your file on life occurrences

- Thoughts on Tragedy and Terror from Carey Nieuwhof - careynieuwhof.com/thoughts-church-age-terror/
- "Talking With Kids About Tragedy" - bradleyhospital. org/talking-kids-about-tragedy

AND, LOTS MORE ...

There are certainly other causes of hurt for families and this list is far from complete. You will think of other categories and you will locate other resources. Continue building your toolkit that you started during this chapter. Share it with others in ministry.

RESOURCES FOR OTHER SITUATIONS TO ADD TO YOUR FILE:

- Imprisonment of a family member - prisonfellowship. org/resources/training-resources/family/
- Big Brothers/Big Sisters of America - bbbs.org/
- "Grief in Times of Crisis" has a ton of additional practical helps and suggestions. Bookmark this or print

out a hard copy for quick reference. lifeway.com/
kidsministry/2013/04/10/grief-in-times-of-crisis/

Finally ... please, please, please do not be overwhelmed with
this list and building your toolkit. In the midst of the thou-
sands of other responsibilities you have, simply take small
steps toward growing your resource file.

Be prayed up. Each day. We never know what opportunities
for ministry to hurting families will occur in any given week.
When you have the opportunity, lean in hard. This may very
well be the BEST chance you'll ever have to minister and love
on that particular family.

Chapter 13

COME ALONGSIDE THE SINGLE PARENT

BY JULIE DEARYAN

THE COLD WIND SLICED THROUGH MY COAT when I got to our specified meeting place at the courthouse. Leah wore tan pants and a worn black sweatshirt. She smiled as I approached. I gave her a hug.

"What do you think is going to happen?" I asked.

She shrugged. "I've been working on this for two years and no one has listened to me yet. I don't know that today is going to help, but I appreciate you coming with me."

"Let's do this," I said.

We walked down the street to the public defender's office where Leah had an appointment. This was the second public defender Leah had tried to see. The first defender she had attempted to meet with had been arrested the week previous for drunk driving. We walked into the office and sat in front of a balding man who looked down most of the time he talked to us. He would try to help, he said, but wasn't sure he could do much.

I shook my head. It seemed like Leah continued to hear this from the court system. Everyone was sorry about Leah's situation, but they didn't know what they could do to help. Leah's finances were tight and her ex-husband didn't pay child support, so she couldn't afford to hire an attorney. Her daughters were 11 and 13. She had left the girls' dad three years before because he was an alcoholic. The girls didn't like going to see their dad but had no choice. He continued to drink excessively and had six DUIs, yet continued to drive. He drove the girls around town without a driver's license with open alcohol in the car. The girls were terrified. Since they attended the church youth program, they had talked to me about their situation. I had tried to help by contacting Juvenile Family Services and also the police department, but nothing seemed to help. Today, we were trying to find out from the public defender what steps we could take next to protect the girls.

After the meeting, I walked back to the courthouse with Leah. I reflected on how difficult it was for many single parents. Situations like this happened often with some of the families I worked with, and it seemed like there was very little real help if the parent didn't have money to fight these things in court. I started working to get to know the local advocacy services, lawyers, and judges to see what I could do to help. But I could see by the tears creeping out of the corner of Leah's eyes that she felt pretty hopeless about protecting her family.

THE SINGLE PARENT

Thom Rainer in a Crosswalk blog highlighted the following statistic. "Three out of ten families with children today in the United States are headed up by a single parent. This makes this group one of the largest population segments in the nation."

Who are the single parents who bring their kids to our ministries? Some are like Leah. They left their spouse for a reason that often involves the safety of their children. If they can't produce concrete proof that their children are in danger, they have to continue to have their children go to the other parent at least every other weekend. This brings stress and frustration which can affect every aspect of their lives.

There are other single parents who have a good relationship with their former spouse and there are those where the children's mother or father might need other types of support. They struggle with even getting to the grocery store or putting dinner on the table. They have to work long hours to compensate for not having other types of financial support.

Sometimes Grandma and/or Grandpa are the single parents. They're raising their grandkids and need the support of our children's ministries as a supplement to what they are trying to do in the home. In our church, we have grandparents who are raising their great-grandchildren. The 6-year-old has dyslexia and behavioral problems and the 5-year-old is manipulative because of being raised by parents who were primarily on drugs. When Great-Grandma brings the children to church, she often just needs some time to restore her own relationship with the Lord. Yet, we've gotten to a point where we often have to ask her to sit with her grandson because he tends to want to hurt other children during class time. What should be a break for her ends up not really being one.

One of our families looked like the perfect family in every way until serious problems started showing up in the marriage. The wife left our church and the dad only had the children every other weekend which left him heartbroken. One week, he came without his children to church which made him feel his loss even more keenly. Also, everything about the church from the lobby to the kids' ministry rooms, made him remember his former happier life with his family. The next week, he would have his children with him and bring them to church. The kids would be so excited to see all their friends at church but frustrated that they no longer could come every week since they had to attend two different churches with each parent.

In one case, we had a man whose wife had died of cancer. The children struggled for a long time afterwards, not knowing how to act or feel. Other single parents don't have much contact with the father or mother of their children and really can feel like they're in it alone. Whatever the case, being a single parent produces unique challenges that we as church leaders need to come alongside and help.

SINGLE PARENT STRESSORS

One of the main stresses in a single parent family can be finances. Raising a family on one income or relying on an ex-spouse for child support can be one of the hardest parts about parenting alone. When we have events for our kids' ministry, we often reduce or waive the fees for the single parent family so they can participate. Also, you can ask families in the church to make meals or bring groceries during times when finances are low. This has the added benefit of helping others in the church be aware of what's going on in other families' lives. It also helps the single parent feel like they are not alone.

Day-to-day duties for a single parent are no different than for 2-parent homes with one vital difference: one person does everything. That person helps the kids get their homework done, get them to and from school, ferry them to and from sports practice, drive them to and from church, nurture them, feed them, support them, and often be both mother and father to them. No wonder they can sometimes feel overwhelmed.

In addition, single parents sometimes deal with disapproval from family members, gossiping coworkers, and yes, even those in the church who judge why the person is single. This should be the last place the single parent feels judgment. But they often do. Why?

They look around and see the church is full of what looks like perfect 2-parent families. They're single but often don't necessarily want to be part of the singles group at church. Most adult groups in the church are made for couples. They want their kids to receive spiritual insight and help from the kids' ministry, but sometimes, because of the demands on their time, they don't have time to bring their kids to the Christmas party or Fall Fest. Or maybe the other parent has the child for an event that's a big deal in your church. The parent then has no child to bring to the family-centered holiday party your church is having. This can make the single parent feel particularly left out of the loop.

HOW TO HELP THE SINGLE PARENT

1. Welcome them.

When the single parent walks in the door, make sure everyone is welcoming. Do what you can to make the person feel as comfortable as possible. When that person brings the child to check into your kids' ministry, be careful with your questions on the form. Show your forms to single parents you already know in your church and ask if the forms are single parent friendly. In your teaching, be careful of lessons that talk about a traditional home with Mom and Dad both present. Think of how that might come across to a child from a broken home.

Be sensitive how you celebrate exclusionary holidays at your church. If a single dad is coming to your church and you have a big Mother's Day event, how will he feel? The same goes for the single mom on Father's Day. Also, be aware of events where you have just the mother and daughter come out. If the mom is raising boys, she feels excluded. No way around that.

2. Identify unique needs.

Single parents have unique needs. Consider that a single mom might be overwhelmed with yardwork around her house.

Could men in your church help with that? How about your teens? Work on finding men in the church willing to mentor the single mom's boys. Also, find women in the church willing to take a single dad's girls out shopping or to lunch. Are there attorneys in the church willing to assist with the legal stuff that arises in a single parent's home? Are there accountants willing to help at tax time? Create a network of services that the single person can access to help with their needs.

3. Provide a support system.

Connect single parents with mentoring couples and other single parents. Have a group of them over to your house for a barbeque or a game night. Offer to babysit so the single moms or dads can just have time for themselves.

4. Relationship is key.

Get to know the single parents and their lives. Take them out to coffee. Try to get into their day-to-day business. Get to know that person's struggles. Be sensitive when you're with them and don't complain about your spouse during every conversation. They would be thankful for a spouse even if it meant they simply had someone to sit in the car with the sleeping kids so they could run into the grocery store alone. Listen with your heart when a single parent is telling you what's going on in his or her life.

Celebrate the smallest victories with them or be a shoulder to cry on when that is needed. Be a friend. Sometimes, they're still trying to pick up the pieces of their lives and all they need is someone to listen and be there for them.

Sarah goes to a church in our area and is raising two preteen boys. She says attending services reminds her she isn't alone. She is also glad to have people to discuss what's going on in her children's lives and to get advice from them.

As the years have gone by, one of the ways I've been able to assist single parents is through being there for them during custody battles and court issues. Navigating the court system can be truly overwhelming. Just simply saying you will be there when they wait in court can be a huge blessing. You don't have to know much about court yourself. All you need to do is be a caring person.

We had met Leah's family by going door-to-door and visiting them at their home. Leah had been sitting at her kitchen table with her three girls trying to figure out what to do next. Her oldest daughter had been dating someone who had tried to commit suicide and the mother of the boy had been calling the daughter saying she needed to do something to help her son. The younger girls were frustrated because they had to be with their dad every other week and he was drinking constantly.

The family started attending our church and children's ministries and all three girls trusted Christ. Things on the spiritual level were going much better for Leah and her girls. But it seemed like she couldn't find protection for her girls.

On the day I went with Leah to meet with the public defender, I had never seen her so discouraged. She didn't have the money to pay for her own attorney and it seemed like in no way could she get protection for her daughters. As we walked back to the courthouse to file paperwork, a juvenile service worker named Mike walked towards us. He smiled when he saw us and asked us how we were doing.

"Not too good," Leah said. She told him about her meeting with the public defender.

"Come into the courthouse with me," Mike said. "I think we finally have some good news for you."

We turned to each other and smiled hopefully. We followed Mike into the courthouse and up the stairs. Once there, we went to the window where the secretary sat for the family court. The judge came into the office and so did some other workers. They all had big grins. They held a paper up to the window. We hurried to see what it said. It was an Order of

Protection against Leah's ex-husband. The girls didn't have to be with their dad every other weekend. Leah's eyes filled with happy tears.

We all hugged each other that day. I thought about my life as a children's ministry worker. I wouldn't have dreamed before I started working in children's ministry that going to court with single parents would be part of my resume but that has turned out to be part of my ministry. I've done this kind of thing for many people throughout the years. Court dates are part of their lives in many ways, and it is one of the many ways we can be a support to them in our churches.

It's important to remember that single parents have many needs and unique issues that they face on a day-to-day basis. I can think of no greater place where they can receive comfort, hope, and help than our local churches and our kids' ministries. Let's make sure we give them the support they need so their children can grow to know, love, and serve the Lord Jesus Christ.

Chapter 14

LAY A SPIRITUAL FOUNDATION IN THE FIRST FIVE YEARS

BY KAL OTIS

A CHILD'S BRAIN DOUBLES IN SIZE in the first year and keeps growing to about 80% of adult size by age three and 90% by age five. Both positive and negative experiences shape how his or her brain develops. What a child hears, sees, touches, smells, and tastes stimulate connections that become foundations for future physical, emotional, intellectual, and spiritual development. All these are linked, and each depends on, and influences the other. When you realize the urgency of setting a strong spiritual foundation for children you must realize that you can't do this alone.

As the Church, we must find ways to encourage and partner with our parents as they engage in the most important role of their lives. After all, according to Ephesians 4:12, God calls parents to serve as the primary spiritual trainers of their child. One way to equip parents (as well as volunteers) is to teach them to leverage the limited and unique opportunities that exist during these years. This has the potential to not only help children know and experience God's unconditional love but also to discover how to relate to Him at every new stage of their lives.

Growing up is hard work and comes with taking a lot of risks. It's important to keep in mind that during the first five years, children feel loved when they feel safe. Safety = Love.

WILL YOU KEEP ME SAFE (LOVE ME) AS I LEARN TO TRUST?

0-1 years old

A baby's inability to take care of him or herself produces unique tensions during the first year. Since babies are solely reliant on others, relationships are experiences that shape the way they see the world. There is a direct link between how caregivers respond to a baby's needs and how children will learn to trust others and ultimately, God. Relationships teach babies whether the world is safe and secure, as well as if they're loved and by whom. It's vital that babies experience strong attachments. These attachments are formed when parents and caretakers consistently take care of a baby's physical needs, which make him or her feel safe. This builds trust.

Parents and volunteers can evoke trust when they:

- Slow down to hold, cuddle, and interact with babies as much as possible.

- Take care of their baby's needs with love.

- Repeatedly share a few biblical truths like "God made (baby's name) and "God loves (baby's name)" in a soft, soothing voice.

- Staff the nursery with consistent volunteers. This elicits trust and comfort in both the mother and baby.

- Ensure babies feel safe and loved while in your nursery. Create a questionnaire so new mothers can provide important information, such as how their babies like to be held, soothed, fed, rocked, and laid down in a crib when sleepy.

- Follow up with parents about their baby's time in the nursery.

- Provide opportunities for new moms to refuel each week, so they're able to give their baby the love they need.

WILL YOU KEEP ME SAFE (LOVE ME) AS I LEARN TO BECOME INDEPENDENT?

1-2 years old

A toddler's growing need for autonomy causes tensions during the second year of life. As toddlers develop physical, mental, and emotional skills, they're discovering that they have a personality, with their own desires and abilities. Adults meanwhile try to cope with this emerging individuality. When we actively nurture toddlers' need for autonomy, we help them gain confidence, which leads to a positive self-image. On the other hand, when we dampen their efforts, we contribute to feelings of shame. Since toddlers identify themselves with these feelings, it's important to help them experience hope at home and in our classrooms.

Parents and volunteers can help toddlers gain confidence when they:

- Accept the fact that this is the "Me-do-it" stage! They will be determined to feed, dress, and complete tasks by themselves. Expect messes and spills. Praise toddlers for their smallest efforts.

- Expect them to be active. Toddlers discover their abilities, as well as the relationship between action and consequences, as they climb, jump, hop, skip, touch, manipulate, and explore their world using all five senses.

- Give them the freedom to safely make choices without correcting them.
- Provide opportunities to observe, experiment, sort (they love matching socks), solve problems, and learn from their mistakes.
- Share Bible stories and songs that engage their imaginations and facilitate role-play.
- Refrain from constant harsh criticism and unrealistic expectations.
- Provide toys and space that allow them to repeatedly fail safely. Use encouraging words and hugs when they fall or struggle so they experience hope.
- Show them acceptable ways to express frustration.
- Child proof your environments to minimize using "No." Constant no's produce shame and self-doubt.

WILL YOU KEEP ME SAFE (LOVE ME) AS I LEARN TO TAKE INITIATIVE?

3-4 years old

The constant physical demands on parents and others begin to slow down as children enter this stage. Now it's time to mentally gear up for a non-stop Q&A session fueled by their increasing curiosity and constant need to know why? As 3- and 4-year-old preschoolers gain increased muscular, mental, and language abilities, they feed their appetite for learning by seeking more activities and posing many difficult questions. They're taking in large amounts of information about the world and putting it all together like a big puzzle.

Life becomes confusing as they increasingly gain independence and build confidence. It's hard to distinguish between acceptable and non-acceptable behaviors. Preschoolers are applauded when they throw a ball to someone but scolded when they throw it at a window. It's acceptable when adults behave in certain ways, but imitating those same behaviors gets preschoolers in trouble. They're learning the rules of life while getting some necessary discipline. When parents answer questions, they reinforce the preschoolers' intellectual initiative. On the other hand, when adults see their questions as a nuisance, they stifle initiative and cause preschoolers to feel ashamed of themselves. This results in toddlers becoming overly dependent on others and feeling guilty about self-initiated activities.

Parents and volunteers can help 3- to 4-year-olds take initiative by:

- Letting them know you still love them by hugging and cuddling them when they make bad choices.

- Guiding them lovingly through a few simple rules in order to demonstrate to them that you can be trusted as they explore their world. They will respond with obedience to the ones who keep them safe.

- Showing them grace after their first attempt of non-acceptable behavior and explaining the consequence they will face if that behavior is repeated.

- Being consistent with expectations and discipline.

- Motivating them by appealing to their strong desire to play and have fun. Turn tasks and activities into games. Engage with them and let them see that you like playing and having fun with them.

- Tirelessly feed their curiosity and answer their why's with simple answers. If they're asking you questions, they know you're safe and that you have the answers. Remember that your expression and tone carries more weight then you realize.

- Give them simple tasks that they can initiate and complete on their own.

- Give them room to fail and then succeed without short-changing their efforts.

- Give them freedom and opportunities to initiate imaginative play so they can explore and reenact the different roles and actions of both real and fictional people.

- Make them feel comfortable initiating role-play. Participate with them. You'll learn a lot about what they're thinking.

- Improve their growing vocabulary by talking to them as much as possible. This will give them the confidence to express what they want and how they feel.

- Share Bible stories that have characters they can identify with, like David and Joseph.

Besides providing parents with information and tips to navigate unique opportunities at each age, the church can also undergird parents in these ways.

Help parents discern what is critical for their child's spiritual formation. Parents are bombarded with all kinds of parenting advice via magazines, television, social media, friends, and family. They experience sleeplessness, exhaustion, and constant busyness. The idea of doing one more thing can be discouraging and stressful. This is why Deuteronomy 6:4-9 exhorts parents to model their love for God in their daily routines which becomes a catalyst in building faith at home. Provide simple resources that equip parents to have faith conversations during bath, drive, meal, and hang times. Emphasize the wisdom in repeating activities since stronger brain connections are made through repetition.

Offer felt-need classes. Every stage of life brings a need to develop a new set of skills. Ask an expert from your church to teach a class on nutrition, potty training, discipline, or other topics, through a biblical filter. Take a minute to share your vision of partnership, and allow time for parents to network.

Create a network of support so parents feel cared for. Provide parents with godly mentors to combat culture from defining a parent's role instead of God's Word. Pair young parents with older parents or grandparents and ask them to share their wisdom. Host events such as Mom's Day Out and play dates.

Equip and celebrate milestones. Help parents anticipate, prepare, and celebrate the next stage of their child's life through a milestone ministry which includes family dedication, my first Bible, etc. Encourage parents by educating them as well as providing practical tools to actively practice their faith in the stage they're in.

There is no greater influence in a child's life than the parent relationship. Research indicates that parents who are well informed during the first five years can prevent potential problems down the road. When you partner with parents, you not only strengthen the foundation of their homes, but also bless the Church.

Chapter 15

SUPPORT THE ADOPTIVE AND FOSTER FAMILY

BY PATRICK MILLER

I WANT YOU TO KNOW that I have prayed for you as you read this. Foster care and adoption is something I have been passionate about since I was in college. My wife and I adopted our son through a private agency at birth and are currently less than a month into fostering our first two kids. Our daily life consists of dirty diapers, toddler tantrums, and lots of love. I wouldn't trade it for anything!

When my wife and I adopted our son, I had a very idealistic mindset. I knew the Bible said in James 1:27 (NLT) that I should be *"caring for orphans and widows"* and I pictured how this process was going to be great ... easy ... perfect.

Maybe that's how some of you picture this process. There were so many things that I was totally wrong about. First off,

I figured our son's birth-mom would be a teenager, not someone my age who already had a couple of kids. Then I thought having a baby shower would be normal, because that's what normal soon-to-be-parents do. That was until we had a baby shower for a child we would never get to see.

After adopting, I thought I would have more realistic expectations about the process for foster care. I was wrong. The day we brought home the two kids we are currently fostering, I couldn't help but think, "Do we really have enough love to give to everyone? Will I be able to bond with these new kids or is my heart guarded, because I don't want to get hurt?"

Fostering and adopting are hard. It takes a special kind of family. I believe that not everyone is meant for this, but I also firmly believe there is something everyone can do to help. I pray that God will open your mind to see ways you can support families in their journey.

ASK QUESTIONS

The first thing I want to challenge you to do is to ask good questions of the foster/adoptive family. Don't settle for just asking, "How's it going?" You may not know what to ask, though. Here is your cheat sheet on some questions to ask about their story.

THE PROCESS

Start by asking about the process. There are so many things that have to be done in the process of fostering or adopting. Usually, there are some things that are very similar: lots of paperwork, background checks, answering what seems like a hundred questions. Maybe you'll find out there's something you can help with.

One of the things my wife and I had to do for our son's adoption was to make a book for the birth-moms to view. It still sounds strange to me even now that this is how someone would choose to place their child with a family. The more you understand about the process, the better you can pray for them.

PARENTING TIPS

Have you ever tried to babysit a 2-year-old who could say some words but most of them you couldn't understand? That's hard on everyone, especially the child who doesn't understand why you're not bringing them their cup. Now imagine fostering a child or adopting a child from another country and your communication is limited. Or maybe the child never had to use words at their previous home. This leads to what a parent would call "unwanted behaviors" from the child.

Behavior isn't just a behavior; it's the way a child communicates. When you have a child with you from birth, you have time to train them how to communicate. When you foster a child, you're trying to learn an entirely new language and sometimes that's hard. Ask the family if they're having a hard time with any of their child's behaviors.

PAINFUL TIMES

Understand that some days are going to be harder than others. You have probably heard of birthing pains, but there are adopting pains that create physical pain, too. My wife had a harder time with this than me, but I remember one night in particular. It was Christmas Eve and another family who was adopting through the same agency we were using saw us walking in the parking lot after the church service. With completely pure and joyful intentions, they said their family had been matched with a birth-mom. We had not. That Christmas Eve was hard. Parent/Child Dedication Sundays, Mother's Day, and Father's Day can all be very hard as well. There are going to be other times that make the waiting process almost unbearable. Send them a text or something to let them know you are thinking about them and praying for their future family.

WORDS AND QUESTIONS TO AVOID

Before I start this section, let me say that nearly everyone who uses these words or asks these questions do not mean any harm. Most of the time, it's how they're trying to find out more information about the process.

"Real parents" or "Kids of your own"

The correct term is "biological parents" or "biological kids." We're our son's real parents. He is our own son. I don't introduce my son as our adopted son. I simply call him my son.

"Now you'll probably get pregnant."

I've heard this one a few times by lots of well-intentioned friends. While there are some stories like this, they are rare.

"Will you adopt the kids you are fostering?"

It's just human nature to wonder what will ultimately happen to the kids who are placed in foster care. It's like a football team that's being asked about their next game. We want to know what will happen next, and God doesn't always want us to know that part. Fostering is a constant reminder not to worry about tomorrow. I don't even know if these kids I have will like the food I give them at dinner. The last thing I'm thinking about is if they will become adoptable.

"Oh! What happened to their parents?"

I love a good story. Most people love a good story. I, most likely, will never share every part of my son's adoption story with you. That's because my son's story is just that, it's his. I love to share some parts of our adoption process, like how God, through the trial of waiting to be matched with a birth-mom, taught me to be humble and to genuinely express my feelings to my Heavenly Father. The same goes for the kids we have in foster care. Their parents are in the process of getting the help they need to become better. The parents' stories and the kids' stories belong to them. It's not my place to share things that might make others look at them as different.

MINISTRY ON A LARGER SCALE

I want to encourage you to use those questions to help you get to know and love families better. I want to also encourage you to share the questions with the leaders in your ministry to help them as well.

There is more to ministering to foster and adoptive parents than just asking the right questions. As a leader, you can set the tone for ministry. The more you support those who foster ... the more you celebrate the families that adopt ... the more people hear about opportunities to love on the kids and families ... the more likely others are to foster and to adopt.

Here are some larger scale ways I want to encourage you to pray about. These are things that I have been involved with or heard about from others. It's my prayer that at least one of these will stand out to you as something God wants you to implement this year.

FOSTER TRAINING HOURS

I'll start with the one I think is the easiest, because it's something you might already be doing. As far as my state, Oklahoma, is concerned, foster parents can get their required hours of training by attending parenting classes or Bible studies at church. I had no clue that a Bible study series on parenting would count as training hours until my wife and I became foster parents. Every state may be different on what is required, but it's something worth looking into.

BIRTH-MOM RETREAT

One of my favorite things that I had the chance to serve at in a very small way was a worship retreat for women who had placed their children for adoption. A local adoption agency presented it. My wife and I simply made cupcakes, boxed them up, and wrote a note of encouragement to them. If you're able to put on a one-day retreat like this, please do it. Get with some of your local adoption agencies and make it happen.

PARTNER WITH AGENCIES

There are other things you can do if you partner with local agencies or other groups that support fostering and adoption. Our foster care agency hosted a luncheon for pastors to share ways the church can be involved in these ministries. The information was great and it was a chance to connect with others who are helping families in their church. I know that some of my favorite ideas and events for anything kids' ministry related have come because it worked well at another church.

FOSTER FAMILY FUN

One of the ideas that came from this luncheon was to have your church host, what they called, Foster Family Fun events. These don't have to be anything elaborate, but just imagine a chance for your foster families to all hang out together and share stories and tips they have learned. It could be a picnic or an outing for ice cream sundaes. Get some others from your church to help out with these events or partner with other churches in your area.

USE HOLIDAYS

I promise not to say that every event I have done was my favorite, but there was another one that I really loved doing. The church hosted a Christmas event for kids in foster care. Weeks before, members of the church were encouraged to buy gifts for the kids, similar to what Angel Tree does at Christmas. My favorite part was when the case workers brought some of the kids to the church for a party. The kids got to open the gifts we bought for them! Use the party as a chance to share the Gospel with the kids. Use it as a chance to share the Gospel with the case workers. Use it as a chance to get people to serve in a very rewarding and a very easy way. Holidays, especially Christmas, are natural times when people at your church are thinking of ways they can give to others. Take advantage of those times to bless families that are fostering.

FOSTER FAMILY DEDICATION

Your church probably does some type of parent/child dedication. Have you thought about doing a parent/child dedication whenever a family gets a new foster placement? Some families might be like me and really dislike being the center of attention, but this is such an exciting way to help others see the kingdom impact of raising children who are not just in state custody but are children of God. Maybe someone at your church will see this family and God will speak to their heart on how they can serve them.

ADOPTION RECOGNITION

You could also do something similar for those who have adopted or have been adopted. One Sunday (Orphan Sunday is usually the second weekend in November and would make a good day for this), have everyone who has adopted or they themselves were adopted come down front for a time of prayer. This shows the church how important it is to seriously consider adopting. Spend time in prayer for these families that God would continue to guide them with any struggles they may face.

WHO WILL GO WITH YOU?

My last idea for you is probably the hardest. Think about someone you know in your church who is passionate about foster care and adoption. Bring them alongside you in this process and equip them to help you manage some of these ideas. All the best sports teams have more than one player who steps up and does more than anyone ever thought they could. Who will be the person God lays upon your heart who will exceed and excel in ministering to the adoptive or foster family?

ENCOURAGEMENT

I believe that God created families to be the primary way that a love for Him is passed along to the world. This chapter started with the verse from James that lists two specific people the church is to care for or look after: the orphans and the widows. These two people are ones who have greater difficulty providing for themselves.

The reason I adopted, the reason I am fostering, and the reason I am invested in kids' ministry is because I want to be someone who stands up for those who cannot stand up for themselves. My role as a parent and your role as a kids' ministry leader is to fight back against Satan ... to fight back against Satan when a marriage is under attack ... to fight back against Satan when a child needs to experience the love of God ... to fight back against Satan because a child can't fight this battle alone.

I know that by myself I will never be able to think of every way to support those fighting for kids. I pray that God will bless the time you spend thinking about ministering to foster and adoptive families. See yourself how God sees you. You are like Aaron and Hur when, in Exodus 17, they held up the exhausted and weary arms of Moses so the Hebrew people could win the battle. You are that person supporting the families, so the battle against Satan can be won.

Chapter 16

BRING ALOHA TO YOUR MINISTRY

BY JAMIE SWOPE

ALOOOOOOOHA!" WOULD BE THE FIRST WORD you'd hear at the opening of a Hawaiian luau, followed by the sight of grass skirts swaying to island songs. Many people know "aloha" to mean a greeting or a goodbye, and they may know it to mean love. But it means far more than that. It's a way of life. And it's something I learned while living in Hawaii that showed me how to do ministry with deeper love and a stronger sense of community.

After a short three years living in Hawaii, the Lord called me into a staff role at a church in our new East Coast community as the Family Ministry Director. The Holy Spirit nudged me to share the love and connectedness my Hawaii friends imparted to me with my new church family, and the Lord blessed that.

ALOHA AND WELCOME

Driving up to a church the first Sunday after moving to Hawaii, my heart skipped a few beats as I viewed a building against the backdrop of the beautiful tropical mountain range that I had only seen in movies like *Jurassic Park* and on computer nature scape screensavers. My awe soon turned to anxiousness. Would this community of believers accept us? Would my child be welcomed? I didn't worry much longer as the children's ministry director saw our daughter, came over, and introduced herself as "Auntie." My husband mumbled to me under his breath "That's a little forward, isn't it?" She then showed us our daughter's Sunday school classroom and brought over "Uncle Dave" to welcome her with a shell lei.

Fast forward to today ... hanging in my closet are approximately 20 leis—most of them made of shells and some made of kukui nuts and beads. Many of those leis were lovingly placed around my neck with a warm greeting from a new island friend. And several of those warm greetings happened as my family visited various church congregations to decide which church the Lord would have us join. In every church we stepped foot in during our time in Hawaii, a leader from the church asked new visitors to stand. On those occasions, I would hesitantly stand as someone rushed over to bring my family leis and to exchange a hug and sometimes a kiss on the cheek.

Like many cultural changes, this became a new normal and routine I looked forward to and adopted as well. I loved being able to tell when it was someone's first day at church because of the lei around his/her neck. And while it may put people on the spot, the lei tradition is normal in Hawaii, and effectively breaks the ice for visitors.

I'm back on the mainland now (Hawaiian talk for the continental United States). Today as a ministry leader, I seek out visitors in the worship services, but I sure miss the leis that gave me a hint that someone is new and could use a warm welcome. While I may not have a lei to give, I try to pass along the same kind of aloha that made me feel so instantly a part of a church community.

Jesus sums it up best with his Sermon on the Mount encouragement found in Matthew 5:46-48 (ESV): *"For if you love those who love you, what reward do you have? Do not even the tax collectors do the same? And if you greet only your brothers, what more are you doing than others? Do not even the Gentiles do the same?"* May we not grow too comfortable with our usual circles of friends to ignore showing love to those we do not yet know.

CULTIVATING OHANA

Days on the island turned into months, and I learned that children on the island are taught to call their elders "Auntie and Uncle." It became vernacular; we used it, too. We also adopted the Hawaiian term "ohana" which directly translates to "family." But this word transcends family in the traditional sense and also communicates a community that loves and cares for each other. This sense of ohana made this place that was so far away from our hometown feel like home. We had many aunties and uncles who became part of our lives. It was no longer a norm to come to a church service and leave to go back to our own lives. Rather, it was an expectation that church family time would continue into a meal shared and stories told.

Hawaiians are known for loving to "talk story" as they call it. They want to know your story and share their own. Through this tightly woven faith community, I was loved, nurtured, and challenged to grow in my relationship with Christ. After three years, my husband received military orders for the East Coast and we left the island. But the island vibes never left our hearts, and we carried our yearning and striving for deeper community to where the Lord led us next.

Within our family and children's ministries, we all hope a visiting family loves our church and chooses to return. But if we're honest, how many of our attenders are truly connected to the church body? How do we encourage an attending family to dive into the community and become a part of the church "ohana"? It starts with an invitation to be part of the family of God. Many churches and leaders are fantastic at systems to invite new attenders to Bible studies and programs and "meet the leader" type of events. But being an active participant is different than being part of the church family. This takes time together outside of the church walls.

When I moved to our current church and took on my staff role, I didn't know a single soul as all of our friends were still back in Hawaii. We craved that community, so we decided we were going to be proactive at making friends. We took our Hawaiian-learned custom of "breaking bread" together after church and started inviting a family we didn't know out to eat or over to our home. The first family we invited included a Sunday school teacher on my team named James who I wanted to get to know better. We had a great meal, our kids became instant friends, and something amazing happened that I couldn't have planned.

James' wife, Michelle, became a dear friend to me. But as we began to spend more time with them, Michelle shared with me that she didn't usually come to church. She let Sundays be a time for the kids to go to church with their dad while she rested because she was overworked and tired. What broke my heart is that church didn't feel like a place where she could find rest in the ultimate Rest-Giver. Michelle didn't have a friend in the church and while she appreciated the sermons and worship time when she did attend, it wasn't much of a community for her. I could tell just by sharing this with me, Michelle was unburdened. Dear Michelle didn't realize that when you become friends with the family ministry director, you're going to find yourself joining in the mission and serving too. I discovered she had amazing organizational and administrative gifts. And what a joy many months later to hear her stand before the church sharing her testimony that choosing to join in the ministry and be an active participant of the church family changed her life for the better. Her walk with the Lord is better for it because she's part of a loving community of believers who spur her on. Hallelujah!

It's a challenge, and actually an impossibility to become dear friends with everyone. But making time to let people be part of your life and be part of their lives opens up an opportunity for the Lord to do incredible things. Going out to lunch with friends each Sunday is still a weekly routine for us. We sometimes plan who we ask to lunch, but most of the time we ask people right after church. And we don't just ask families. Our last lunch out, around the table sat a retired couple in their 60s, a single woman in her 70s, a newly married couple in their early 20s, and a single young lady in her 30s. We weren't necessarily being intentional to have such a hybrid of ages, but it's naturally a blended community because we've cultivated a sense among our church family that we are all one big extended family, inter-generationally. My children ran around the sandwich shop that day, chatting the ear off of the retired couple who had quickly become like surrogate grandparents for our military children who live far away from their own grandparents. Who knew I'd find a sense of ohana after our Hawaii days? God did, and to Him all the glory. Who will you break bread with this week?

Play dates with moms and dads in the family ministry has become another personal touch and way to connect. There is just not enough time on a Sunday morning to learn a lot about each other. A woman named Jessica called our church one day to speak with someone about our children's program. When I returned her call she shared that she wanted to bring her young children to church to get a "Christian education." She also bravely explained she didn't know one thing about God or how to do the church thing. And she wasn't planning on becoming "religious." But her husband was raised a Christian, and she was trying to support him. My evangelism tentacles grew out of my head and the Holy Spirit gave me the courage to tell her this: "You are doing a wonderful thing bringing your children to church. There will likely be times when you hear something in the sermon or in a song that stirs you and raises questions. I haven't even met you yet, but I want you to know that there is no question too strange or too forward you can't ask me." And then I invited her to a playdate. Their family began attending regularly. Playdates turned into weekly get-togethers to talk about the Bible and who Jesus is. After about 5 months of time sharing our lives and being transparent, Jessica "confessed with her mouth Jesus Christ is Lord" and the angels rejoiced!

My Hawaiian friends taught me how "talking story" can draw people together and allow the Holy Spirit to do incredible things in hearts. I would encourage you to put people ahead of tasks and make it routine to spend time with those you serve in a context that works for you. Play dates are easy for me because of the age of my children. Sharing a cup of coffee in your office works just as well. Reach out to a few people this week and make a plan to get together outside of church meeting times.

ALOHA AND GOODBYE

How thankful I am for the season of tropical palm trees, pineapple juice, and warm ocean swims. And oh, how I miss those days. But I'm so amazed by our Heavenly Father who gave me an even greater gift during that season of life. He taught me how to love deeper. The aloha ways I learned kindled within my heart a desire to know people better and be a true sister (or Auntie) in Christ. My prayer for you, co-laborer for Christ, is that the Lord sparks in you an aloha passion to share His love.

Chapter 17

LISTEN TO YOUR PARENTS: QUESTIONNAIRE

BY ROB LIVINGSTON

Have you ever desired to help parents connect with their kids but just didn't know where to start? This questionnaire will help give you a foundation for each family in your ministry and allow you to minister to each family where they are in life. Just like each individual is not the same, families in your ministry have differences, as well. It is important to know each family's demographic so you can minister to them in the best possible way. This is by no means an exhaustive list of questions but a set of questions that will hopefully start you down the path of success.

PARENT QUESTIONNAIRE

Basic Personal Info

Mom's Name _____

Dad's Name _____

Mom's Cell Phone _____

Dad's Cell Phone _____

Mom's email _____

Dad's email _____

What is the best way to get in touch with you? (email, phone call, text, Facebook messenger)

Mom _____

Dad _____

How many children do you have and what are their ages?

Child 1 _____ Age: ___

Child 2 _____ Age: ___

Child 3 _____ Age: ___

Child 4 _____ Age: ___

Does your child attend public school, private school, or homeschool? _____

Do they participate in any extracurricular activities. If so, what? _____

_____

_____

Where do you work? _____

_____

How many hours a week do you work? _____

Which of the following social media networks are you and your child active with? (include your user name)

Facebook: _____

Instagram: _____

Twitter: _____

Snapchat: _____

How often do you sit down as a family and eat a meal together?

Never   1-2 times per week

3-4 times per week   5+ times per week

What would you say is your biggest struggle as a parent raising your children?

_____

_____

_____

_____

Church/Bible

On a scale of 1 to 10 (1 being not at all and 10 being completely comfortable) answer the following questions.

How comfortable are you talking about the Bible with your child? _____

How comfortable are you leading your child to Christ? _____

How comfortable are you praying out loud with your child? _____

How many years have you been attending church?

    1 year or less   2 – 4 years

    5-8 years   10+ years

How often do you attend church as a family?

Every time doors open   twice a week

once a week   once a month

How many Bibles do you have in your home? _____

How often do you read your Bible during the week?

   Daily   1-2 times a week   3-4 times a week

   5-6 times a week

How often do you pray during the week?

   Multiple times a day   once a day

   just before eating   What's prayer?

Do you pray together as a family during the week? If so, how often?

      Yes _____   No _____

When you miss church, which of the following is the closest reason why?

   Family vacation

   Travel sports

   lack of interest

   other _____

If the church/children's ministry could help you in one way, what would it be?

_____

_____

_____

_____

While some of these questions are self-explanatory, let's talk about how the answers to a few questions can help build your ministry. Let's start with the personal and contact information. It's important to know how to communicate with parents and having the correct contact information is crucial in emergency situations. It's also important to know the parents' contact information to send newsletters, camp letters, and general ministry updates.

The number of children and their ages plays a huge part in how you can minister to the entire family. It is important to know if a child is an only child or one of many. This also helps ministers relate to families better by allowing them to see the entire family dynamic, instead of just the one or two that may be in the given ministry area.

When it comes to where children go to school and what activities they are involved in, this can really help ministers connect and build relationships with the child and the family. This information allows the opportunity, if your community schools permit, to be able to visit each child's school and spend time visiting one-on-one during their school lunch time. By knowing what extracurricular activities they participate in, you can make plans to go watch plays or sporting events. By knowing where kids are spending their time, you can come alongside parents and get to know their interests and hobbies.

Parents' work schedule is important to know for a few reasons. First, it is important to know, so that if or when you make home visits you can be sure not to visit when parents are not there or, even worse, not to visit if they're trying to rest for a night shift. Secondly, it's important to know their work schedule to possibly plan around schedules for certain events. Lastly, it helps paint the bigger picture for the entire family and the dynamic gives a starting point in conversations.

The world is quickly becoming social and you need to keep up with the times. This is why it's important to know what social media platform both the parents and children are using. Connecting through social media will also help keep parents and children connected to the church and what's going on both inside and outside particular ministries.

If you find out that the majority of your families are not sitting at a table eating meals together you can utilize that information to help plan specific lessons or training on the power of eating meals together. There are various tools available to help motivate and encourage parents to have meaningful conversations with their children around a meal. This can also be used to help teach parents that taking the time to sit down with the entire family shows the kids that they are important and parents are willing to put the time into talking and listening to them.

The last question is open ended for a reason. This question allows parents to honestly share some of their struggles with you, which allows you to almost create an individualized family plan of ministry.

When looking at the church and Bible questions, it is important to note that the goal is not to make parents feel like they're not doing a great job. The goal is to learn where they are honestly and step alongside to help them be the best spiritual leaders of their children they can be.

The first three questions address the parent's comfortability level with God's Word, prayer, and leading their child to Christ. These are all areas that you as a children's ministry leader will be asked about throughout the years, so it's a good idea to get a base for where parents feel they are.

To go along with that question, we asked the frequency question to determine how many "touches" we will receive for each child. Another talking point from this question brings up the amount of time a child spends with their parents versus the time they spend at church. We are in a society that relies on the professionals to do a lot of jobs for us, even though we could've done the same thing by ourselves. Parents bring their kid to church for the church to raise them spiritually, but you can carefully remind parents there are 168 hours in a week and if they come every time your doors are open they will only be there 3 of those 168 hours. This is not enough time to build a solid foundation for anyone, especially a child.

The number of Bibles in the house and if the parent is reading their Bible at home can be very influential as the child grows up. Having a Bible readily available and the example of someone reading the Bible can greatly affect how children perceive the Bible in their adult life. Just like Bible reading is important, so too is a healthy prayer life. By praying with your family, you are showing them that God is important and that talking to your Heavenly Father daily is important. It is also important to model how to pray so that when they get older they understand this wonderful opportunity to call on the Lord.

When a family misses church for whatever reason it's good for the staff to know why they are missing, so they can minister to those kids where they are. Kids will miss church for various reasons, but if you know ahead of time, you can create a little devotion to go with them on vacation or to the travel ball game. Just because a child can't make it to church does not mean you should disown or neglect the child. You should use every opportunity to reach these families where they are, and if that means you have to spend some time making extra devotion books, so be it.

The last question is one that you have to pray about before sending it out. You never want to ask parents how you can help and not actually look at the information. Parents want to know they have a voice in what happens with their child at church. Does this mean that every suggestion needs to be made a reality? No, but what it does do is allow parents to be honest with you and tell you where they are struggling and how you can encourage and help.

As we said before, this is not an exhaustive list of questions. Feel free to add or take away, to make this parent survey relevant to the church you serve.

Family Events

Browse these ideas for events that lead families to spiritual growth. Then, devise a plan of how you will provide opportunities for families to have fun, engage in meaningful conversations, and build strong relationships, while growing closer to the Lord ... together.

CHRISTMAS CAROLING OUTREACH

by Cindy Melenric
Well of Life Church, Houston, TX

Every year our family connects with our youth group and their families to lead a Christmas Caroling party event the week before Christmas Day. We schedule a day, meet for refreshments, hand out caroling books, review our route, and head outdoors. We spend about two hours knocking on doors in hope of bringing Christmas cheer. We choose to sing traditional Christmas carols that bring out the true meaning of the season. Other tips would include taking along hard candies, bottled water, flashlights, and strollers for the little ones. Living in Houston, and going through Hurricane Harvey, we chose to minister in hard hit areas. Anyone can do the same in their community or in their own neighborhood.

PRAYING IN THE NEW YEAR

by Ellen Haley
FaithFit Ministries, Austin, TX

Copy one set of prayer prompt strips for each family. The prayer strips should contain elements of praise, thanksgiving, confession, petition, and intercession. Cut the strips and place them in a container (such as a Chinese take-out box or boot mug). Make these available to families at a service prior to New Year's Day. Make a big deal out of it and advertise. Then encourage the families to pray.

At homes, families should place their prayer strip container at the center of their dinner table. Each day at one meal some-one draws out a prayer strip and the family prays together over what is on the strip.

BIBLE COOKS COMPETITION

by Ellen Haley
FaithFit Ministries, Austin, TX

Before the session, go through lists of foods mentioned in the Bible and choose a recipe that would be made using those foods. Replace the words for the food in the recipe with the scripture reference where that food is mentioned.

As families enter assign them a cooking station where they will set up, using the utensils they've brought from home. After everyone has arrived, pass out a sealed copy of the recipe and a Bible in the translation needed for the recipe.

As the timer begins, each family will open their recipe and read through it. Using the Bible provided, families will look up the scripture verses and determine what foods they need. They will then access the "pantry" of foods that are available, taking only what they need. Each member of the family partic-ipates in preparation of the recipe. When the timer goes off, all hands must be off. Judges will check to make sure the families have all the correct ingredients and it is done properly. The other families should continue because finishing first is not the only prize. Judges will taste the foods and present awards.

Here's a sample recipe.

Ingredients

4 or 5 Luke 11:12 (1 per person) - **eggs**

1/4 c. Exodus 3:8 - **milk**

1/4 c. 2 Samuel 17:29 - **cheese**

1/4 t. Ezekiel 43:24 - **salt**

Leviticus 2:13 to taste – **season (pepper)**

1 T. Exodus 29:40 – **oil**

Cooked Mark 5:11 as desired – **pig (bacon & sausage)**

1 Exodus 12:39 per child – **unleavened bread (tortilla)**

Directions

Crack the Luke 11:12s (eggs) into a large bowl. Add Exodus 3:8 (milk) and pre-grated 2 Samuel 17:2 (cheese). Beat thoroughly with a fork. Add Ezekiel 43:24 (salt) and Leviticus 2:13 (seasoning, pepper). Continue to beat until well mixed.

Preheat a skillet and pour in Exodus 2:40 (oil), making sure it coats the bottom and side of pan. Pour Luke 11:12 (egg) mixture into skillet, stirring until cooked. Empty onto a plate.

Each child should help themselves to some precooked Mark 5:11 (pigs—sausage and bacon) and 1 Exodus 12:39 (unleavened bread—tortilla). Place the cooked Luke 11:12 (eggs) on the Exodus 12:39 (unleavened bread—tortilla). Top with Mark 5:11 (pigs—sausage and/or bacon) and extra 2 Samuel 17:2 (cheese). Top with the special topping the workshop leader provides, if desired.

BOOKS BEFORE BEDTIME

by Lisa Davis
Alderwood Community Church, Lynnwood, WA

An event that can help families understand the importance of reading and storytelling is to hold a Books Before Bedtime event. Get your amazing storytellers to come out for a night. Theme the rooms for extra fun: camping, snow, and castle. Kids come in their pajamas, drink hot cocoa, and listen to stories of their choice on a rotating basis. Include book related crafts such as: bookmarks, bookworms, book lights, Bible cases. Provide parents with a quality list of books to read at bedtime.

S'MORES FAMILY PRAYER NIGHT

by Lucinda Gibson
First Baptist Church, Breman, GA

This event is set up in four stations that can be visited in any order. Decorate the four stations with the items to build a s'more. Families will collect s'more items at each station or you can have a separate s'more station to visit after going to the other stations.

- Station 1: Adoration. Write words that describe God on a giant paper graham cracker.

- Station 2: Confession. Family members write sins they are confessing on paper marshmallows. Pray and ask God's forgiveness then toss sins into a fire pit.

- Station 3: Thanksgiving. Families use sidewalk chalk on the sidewalk or parking lot to write or draw things they are thankful for.

- Station 4: Supplication. Write prayer requests on paper Kisses and place them in a candy bowl.

After experiencing the prayer stations, everyone gathers around the fire pits to make s'mores and enjoy time together.

FAMILY BOARD GAME NIGHT

by Rob Livingston
Chapel Hill Baptist Church, Northport, AL

Take a break from the fast-paced social media life and slow down as a family. Bring your favorite board game to church for a night of laughter and excitement. Snacks and extra games will be provided by the church. During the night, take a few family connection breaks to see how God's Word can be seen even in the simplest games.

About halfway through the night have everyone stop and share a mid-event devotion using the board game Trouble. Read John 14:1 aloud. Families will discuss around the table a time when they were worried or "troubled" about a particular situation. Encourage each group to discuss and one of the adults close in prayer.

Continue game night, possibly switching games or tables. As the night comes to a close share 1 Corinthians 8:6 while holding up a deck of UNO cards. Encourage families to be as honest as possible, and share a time they allowed something else to get in their way of putting God first. Close in prayer and encourage families to schedule family game night in their home

SLIP AND SLIDE EVENT

by Sharma Seibert
Clough United Methodist Church, Cincinnati, OH

Our church has an amazing sledding hill! People from all around the community come to use it when it snows. Seeing how popular this is, we decided to try a slip and slide on our sledding hill in the summer. We use a plastic tarp for the slip and slide and use tube-a-loons filled with water to keep the tarp in place. The slip and slide ends up being about 100 feet long going down our sledding hill. This past summer we had the local Fire Department come and use their hoses for the water. Kids and parents love this event, and it brings people in from all around the community.

We also have a bounce house set up and other games that families can do together. We grill hotdogs and supply drinks. It's a blast for the whole family!

EASTER UNDER CONSTRUCTION

by Shawn Howell
PrayerLights YouTube Channel, Rock Hill, SC

Easter Under Construction is a family event that prepares families for the resurrection of Jesus through a station model. Set up this event in a large, open room where families can move about freely. The goal is to have families focus on the events leading up to Easter and to have them work together as a family. Here is one station suggestion, but plan for 4 or 5 total stations.

Lent-To-Go Bags – Each family will put together a bag to guide them through Lenten spiritual practices. Provide brown paper craft bags with an instruction sheet attached to each bag. Include smooth river stones to write a habit that needs changed. Set out chenille sticks for children to form into a stick figure to represent Christ. Draw a cross on paper plates to talk about Jesus' last supper with his friends. Precut small squares of rough burlap cloth to talk about the sadness of Jesus' death on the cross.

Meet The Writers

Michelle Bowen serves as the Director of Ministry Resources for Global Children's Network. As a homeschool mother, kidmin leader, and conference speaker, she is devoted to equipping others in leading children and youth to follow Jesus.

Joy Canupp served as Children's Minister for 15 years in a SC church and has recently transitioned to equipping/encouraging folks in ministry through speaking and blogging at *Leading With Joy*. She loves spending time with family and friends, thrifting, playing games, and all things purple!

After leading Children's Ministries in Houston churches for 30+ years, **Pat Conner** has recently relocated to Central Texas. Now she focuses on writing, consulting, and being Nana to 8 grandchildren and assorted granddogs, grandrabbits, and grandgoats.

Julie Dearyan works with kids and their parents in Fresno, OH. She has been published in *Focus on the Family* and other publications.

Lucinda Gibson serves as Director of Preschool Ministries at First Baptist Bremen in Bremen, GA. She looks up to her husband and father of her 3 daughters, especially since he's a foot and a half taller than her.

After 36 years in kidmin, **Jack Henry** is more passionate than ever to serve! Married for 36 years, he has 2 beautiful children who both love the Lord!

Steven Knight is the Family Life Pastor at Fellowship Bible Church in Waco, TX and the founder of KidminTools.com. He enjoys equipping ministry leaders almost as much as he enjoys a good cup of coffee.

Rob Livingston is the Children's and Recreation Minister at Chapel Hill Baptist Church in Northport, AL ... Roll Tide! He loves all things Disney, traveling, spending time with the kiddos, and doubles as a school bus driver. Watch out for the guy driving a bus with a crazy hat if you're ever in Northport!

Patrick Miller is the Associate Children's Minister at First Moore Baptist Church in Moore, OK. In between the diaper changes, snack times, and episodes of *Peppa Pig*, he and his wife enjoy spending time together camping and watching the Food Network.

Makinna Morrison, 20, is the Director of Children's Ministry at Woodward Avenue Baptist Church in Muscle Shoals, AL. When she isn't working with kids you can find her studying to get her elementary education degree or spending time with family.

Brittany Nelson is the founder of Deeper KidMin, an online resource that equips ministry leaders to grow kids deeper in their relationships with Christ through engaging and affordable ideas. In her spare time, she enjoys reading, chocolate, tea, yoga, and she wants to someday run the Disney Princess Half Marathon dressed as her favorite princess, Belle.

With 30 years of ministry experience, **Kal Otis** currently serves as the Pastor of Family Ministries at South Park Church in Illinois. Her child development background and love for scriptures fuels her passion to equip and empower volunteers, as well as parents, to make the most of spiritual teachable moments when they naturally occur at each stage of development. Blog: kalotis.com

Amber Pike is a children's minister and mom of 2 in LaGrange, KY. She spends her days homeschooling her son, caring for her daughter, and writing during nap time.

Holly Roe is a ministry innovator, consultant, event planner, and coach, and can be contacted through her website, hollyroe.org. She's also the owner/operator of a cinnamon roll bakery in Knoxville, TN called Cinnaholic.

Jamie Swope directs children and family ministry at Neelsville Presbyterian Church in Germantown, MD. She is a proud Army wife to her husband, Kevin, and loves quality time with her 3 kids.

Trish Weeks is the former children's pastor at Tree of Life Church in New Braunfells, TX. Most kidmin do not hold a third-degree black belt in karate, but Trish does ... and it comes in handy sometimes!

As the NextGen Pastor at Sugar Grove Church of Christ in Meadows Place, TX, **Dana Williams** is helping parents raise a generation of kids who are for God and for neighbor because of the Gospel. She's fairly confident that she could survive on tacos (if push came to shove), and she's one of the rare ones who loves having her house full of teenagers!

HOME GROWN

CPSIA information can be obtained
at www.ICGtesting.com
Printed in the USA
FFOW04n0228250218
45247103-45851FF